The Religious Reawakening In America

BOOKS by U.S.NEWS & WORLD REPORT

Joseph Newman—Directing Editor

A division of U.S.News & World Report, Inc.
Washington, D.C.

The Religious Reawakening In America

Contents

Illustrations

Acknowledgments

The editors are indebted to *Gerald S. Snyder* for undertaking the research and the writing of the manuscript for *The Religious Reawakening in America*. Linda S. Glisson edited the manuscript.

A word of appreciation also is due to the following individuals and organizations for their help in gathering material for this book:

Dr. Martin E. Marty, University of Chicago; Edward E. Plowman, *Christianity Today;* Dr. Gerald J. Jud, United Church of Christ; Dr. James H. Cone, Union Theological Seminary, New York City; The Rev. Andrew M. Greeley, University of Chicago; Dr. James H. Pyke and Dr. John H. Satterwhite, Wesley Theological Seminary, Washington, D.C.; Prof. J. Deotis Roberts, Sr., Howard University, Washington, D.C.; Finley P. Dunn, Jr., Temple for Understanding, Washington, D.C.; Rabbi Abraham J. Heschel, Jewish Theological Seminary, New York City; Miss Young Oon Kim and Neil Winterbottom, the Holy Spirit Association for the Unification of World Christianity (Unification Church); Rabbi Eugene Borowitz, Hebrew Union College-Jewish Institute of Religion, New York City; Rabbi Eugene J. Lipman, Temple Sinai, Washington, D.C.; Dr. John Livingood, Robert Agus, and Jim Miller, Washington, D.C.; Mrs. Jean Byrd, Silver Spring, Maryland; Mrs. Lydia Little, Potomac, Maryland.

Agape House, Washington, D.C.; Fabrangen, Washington, D.C.; B'nai B'rith; National Council of Churches; Catholic University of America; Home Missions Board, Southern Baptist Convention, Atlanta, Georgia; The United States Catholic Conference; Synagogue Council of America; The Union of American Hebrew Congregations; The International Society for Krishna Consciousness.

Introduction

At a time when established religion has become an object of criticism, we have moved into what many consider to be one of the most religious periods in the history of the United States.

Young people particularly have sparked the revival of interest in spiritual values. Unfulfilled by the offering of the traditional church and the traditional temple, they have slipped into rebellion—not against God and religious values but against the "establishment" of Christian, Jewish, and other faiths. They are searching for new forms and ways of achieving spiritual satisfaction to offset the dulling and sterile effect of a highly materialistic and technological society.

This book falls into two parts—Challenge and Response. The challenge is clear: the claim that traditional Christianity and traditional Judaism are no longer responding to demands of this modern age. It is, of course, easier to challenge than it is to respond, and in many cases, as one religious leader puts it, the "enemy," the establishment, is what holds the challengers together.

The response is less clear and less obvious, and it cannot be classified easily. The section dealing with this aspect focuses on the fundamental reasons for the behavior of the traditional elements in the major faiths.

Above all, when there is so much confusion, this book seeks to provide an overview of the entire field and to explain what is happening. It is not another "Jesus book," but a treatment of all the major groups and movements which have stirred the religious world.

Does all the noise we hear herald a genuine religious revival? Will the new kinds of interest fade away, or will they endure? What effect will they have on traditional religion as we have known it? What is the outlook for religion?

Some of the answers will be found in this book.

PART ONE

The Challenge

CHAPTER ONE

A New Look at Religion

In the late 1960s, a small group of theologians said God was dead. Throughout America, there was religious unrest. The churches were facing a crisis. Attendance was down. The age of technology and urbanization was causing more and more people to question ancient doctrines. There were efforts to "modernize" faith and to seek more church involvement in great social issues.

Although there was a "rumor" going around that God was alive, a central issue of faith was the nature and even the exist-ence of a supreme being. As one spokesman for the "death of God" theory put it: "We are not simply saying that modern man is incapable of believing in God, or even that we exist in a time in which God has chosen to be silent. We are saying that God has disappeared from history . . . He is truly absent, not simply hidden from view, and therefore he is truly dead."

Today, who would deny that God is alive? The churches are still facing a crisis—greater, some say, than ever before; attendance is still down, and sliding even further; there is an enormous amount of religious unrest; and the questioning of traditional church practices continues as always. But there is today a growing awareness of God. We no longer hear that "God is dead." Instead we hear the 1970s described as the dec-ade of evangelical revival.

We also hear of plans, announced by the nondenominational Campus Crusade for Christ, to contact every home in the

15

United States by 1976. And another project, called Key 73, tells us there will be a "Christian blitz" in America in 1973.

At secular universities, religion is the fastest growing field of graduate study, ahead of any language, ahead of philosophy, of geology, of art, of music, of speech. Clergymen used to be the only ones who went for doctoral degrees, but today more and more young people are studying religion either for personal reasons or to become teachers. A major study of religion graduate programs, sponsored by the American Council of Learned Societies, revealed the following:

> The field of religious studies has been rapidly broadening to include much more than was traditionally assumed as the core of professional studies and to overcome the restriction of study to a single tradition, such as Jewish studies, Christian studies, or Buddhist studies. . . . The new identity in religious studies is marked by definite changes in the objects and patterns of study. These include growing attention to the religious traditions outside the Judeo-Christian orbit—notably the religions of Far Eastern origin, Islam, and primitive religions. The range of religious phenomena is being rapidly expanded to include far more than belief systems, rites, and behavior patterns traditionally called religious.

It is not just the emphasis on study that is new. The approach is also different. Traditionally it was the history and theology of the Bible that drew most of the attention. Now doctoral students must become acquainted with Eastern, Near Eastern, and African faiths. Moreover, religion departments are no longer found only in church-related institutions; they are found in both private schools and in nonsectarian public colleges and universities.

Although there is a revival of interest in religion, the statistics for church and synagogue attendance do not reflect it. In a 1971 Gallup Poll, it was found that only 40 percent of adults of all faiths attend a place of worship in a typical week. This was the lowest percentage reported since these polls were first introduced in 1955. That year the overall percentage for church and synagogue attendance was 49 percent. The percentage has been steadily declining ever since. For instance, in

1959 it was 47 percent, 46 percent in 1962, 45 percent in 1964, 43 percent in 1968, and 42 percent in 1970.

The most pronounced decline has been among Roman Catholics. On the average, according to Gallup, 71 percent of all Catholics attended church regularly in 1964. In 1971 the percentage for a typical week had dropped to 57 percent; in the same year it was 37 for Protestants and 19 for Jews.

Gallup gives the following major church attendance percentages for 1971:

Catholic	57	High school	40
Protestant	37	Grade school	41
Jewish	19	21-29 years old	28
Men	35	30-49 years old	42
		50 & over	45
Women	45	East	39
White	40	Midwest	40
Nonwhite	44	South	45
College-educated	40	West	33

Then there are the high "drop out" figures of the clergymen themselves. There is no exact figure available, but an estimated 3,500 to 17,500 clergymen, or between 1 and 5 percent of the total number, are known to resign each year. In addition, according to a Gallup Poll, many other clergymen have given serious thoughts to resigning—33 percent of them Protestant, 23 percent Roman Catholic and 43 percent Jewish. Among clergymen under the age of forty, the percentages are much higher.

An inability to communicate with people was the main reason given by clergymen of all faiths. Secondary reasons for considering resignation were financial for Protestant clergymen, a desire to marry for Catholics, and a lack of interest for Jews. However, no one reported a complete loss of faith.

Thus, while outward signs of religious interest are growing —as indicated by such movements as the Jesus People and the vigorous interest in religion on the nation's campuses— there is a definite move away from organized religion on the part of many young people. And since the younger generation is on the increase, this is alarming. By 1975, it is estimated, there will be some 235 million people in the United States, and about 50 percent of them will be twenty-five or younger.

Many of today's youth dislike organized religion because they feel that the church and the synagogue are not responding rapidly enough to social and world problems. Required chapel services at some church-affiliated schools are being protested as are conventional religion courses. But this is not to say that young people have lost their religious values. They have not. Religion in the youth culture has a twofold nature. Youths are not going to church regularly and the church is often rejected entirely, but spiritual values are not discarded. As the chaplain at a Seventh-Day Adventist school said, "There is a general enthusiasm for a strong religious commitment to Christ on our campus; at the same time there is a feeling that the church is not quite with it, that it is not meeting the needs of society in a way it ought to."

In his book *New Gods in America*, Peter Rowley suggests that people who seek out "new" religions are "seeking an answer to what seems to them a frightening world."

He further states:

> The old religions are unsatisfying to many. Meaningless ritual, adherence to outmoded rules, hypocritical clergy—all of these are charges thrown against Roman Catholicism, Judaism, and Protestantism. The failure of some organized churches to adapt to the times ... has left the young with little alternative but to seek elsewhere. Drugs, with their inherent threat to health and concentration on selfish sensation, fail also. As does the hippie movement with its too-formless emphasis on love.

Taken as a whole, the religious revival is a complex phenomenon, and no simple attempt to classify it as a "return to religion" will do. The reasons for what is happening are numerous and diverse, reasons that stem in part from the modern cult of technology.

This is the age of dizzying change, of technological invention, of automation and computerization. There has always been change of course, but the rapid change we face today is

YOU HAVE A LOT TO LIVE

JESUS

HAS A LOT TO GIVE

Although many of today's youth are turning away from established religions, they are not rejecting spiritual values.

unprecedented. It is occurring so rapidly in fact that many people feel unprepared to cope with it. Alvin Toffler calls this *Future Shock* and describes it as a disease, a socio-psychological illness brought on by the premature arrival of the future. In his book he warns:

> Future shock will not be found in *Index Medicus* or in any listing of psychological abnormalities. Yet, unless intelligent steps are taken to combat it, millions of human beings will find themselves increasingly disoriented, progressively incompetent to deal rationally with their environments. The malaise, mass neurosis, irrationality, and free-floating violence already apparent in contemporary life are merely a foretaste of what may lie ahead unless we come to understand and treat this disease.

Evidence that change is occurring so rapidly can be found in the fact that 90 percent of all the scientists and engineers who have ever lived are alive today and that the sum of human knowledge is constantly doubling. Knowledge just a few years old is fast becoming obsolete. The boundaries between countries are being torn down; jet planes are shrinking distances; and tools such as the computer are extending man's ability to think. Biochemical advances are improving people's health. But as a result of all this, man's environment and his style of life are radically being changed.

How much longer can we go on multiplying and industrializing? Some scientists concerned with the earth's environmental system claim that there is a "crisis level" and that it may be only forty or fifty years away.

According to one scientist, Professor Jay Forrester, who is a pioneer in system dynamics at the Massachusetts Institute of Technology (MIT), there is a circular process going on among earth's interacting forces in which even birth control and technology may not help. The professor developed a computer model of the world under the sponsorship of the Club of Rome, a group of the world's most eminent social scientists. He found that the interaction of forces of population, industrialization, food supply, natural resources, and pollution could result in a crisis point before the end of the twentieth century.

For instance, he maintains that a lower birth rate that results in more food and capital investment could increase pollution and encourage a rise in the birth rate in order to take advantage of the increased food. If technology produced substitutes to take the place of the shrinking supply of raw materials, this too, says Professor Forrester, would encourage greater capital investment and a higher birthrate and thus cause another pollution crisis. Even if scientists devise sophisticated ways to reduce pollution, this could lead to greater capital investment— and a higher birthrate. And a higher birthrate would mean more pollution. Professor Forrester maintains that the only way to break the circle is through a deliberate planned decline in agricultural and industrial investment that would stop population growth.

Although there are many who challenge the predictions that man's existence is imperiled by overpopulation and industrial growth, the widespread discussion in the media about the possible collapse of society has frightened many young people and explains in part the upsurge of religion among today's youth. As the chaplain at one large university put it: "Young people are convinced that there is going to be a reversion of pollution and we are going to be asphyxiated; this enormous emphasis on ecology has set a lot of them off. A lot of kids honestly believe that the end is going to come."

There are other reasons why thousands of American youth are turning to religious expression. One of the most important is psychological.

Dr. John Livingood, a psychiatrist for the U.S. Public Health Service working at the National Institutes of Mental Health (NIMH) takes this personal view:

> In terms of classic psychology or classic psychiatry, every individual really wants to be very dependent upon a greater power, and as a child that greater power is your parent. You grow up feeling very comfortable at home. It is a deep emotional thing. Thus, on the one hand you have the young wanting to rebel and on the other you have them wanting to go toward something which is going to give them comfort. Christianity, for instance, has provided this for many, many people—God the Father, literally.

Another thing that highlights the youth movements of the last ten years has been a sort of "tribal" getting together. The old religions were losing the appeal of doing things together. Nowadays when you go to church, you do not really contact anybody, you go and sit quietly in the pew and the minister talks, but you do not have any community feeling. Once upon a time, traditional religion did have this. Today this has been lost in America and regardless of what they are into, young people are involved in getting together as a community; in all of the modern movements, you do get a feeling of belonging and working together as a team.

The idea of teamwork is particularly interesting, for much of this new religious interest cuts across denominations; there is no established religion that is not somehow affected, be it traditional Roman Catholicism, mainstream Protestantism, or the three branches of organized Judaism. In some cases there is a new spirit of ecumenism. Both Protestants and Catholics have joined the "Jesus People" movement. There are some Protestants in the "Catholic Pentecostal Movement," and some Christians report finding spiritual alliance with Jews who meet outside of the established synagogue. On college campuses, the ecumenical spirit is particularly strong. "It stems in part from the lack of interest by students in strictly denominational activities," one observer noted. "It comes also from the liberal attitudes of the chaplains. On some campuses these alliances serve mainly as clearinghouses for ideas and problems. But more frequently they have led to joint sponsorship of all campus religious programs."

The spirit is there, but again, there are many who are concerned that it not be misinterpreted. David L. Warren, for one, a member of the Religious Ministry at Yale University, has cautioned in *Commonweal* magazine against the tendency to draw any conclusion that today's youth have returned to the fold of old-time religion:

The hope against hope which is being voiced from the pulpit is that American college youth have come home again, that they have returned to the fold of American Culture Religion as it has been practiced for the last 25 years. . . . There is a religious revival going on but it is in almost dialectic tension with the whole spirit and law of the dominant church in America. . . . Depending on the orientation of the individual, Jesus might become a model for the Socratic Teacher, Drop-Out Carpenter, Prototype of Civil Disobedience, Liberator of His People, Mystery Man, Moral Authority, Faith Healer or Communal Organizer. . . . Rather than returning to the fold, many of these young people have apparently rejected the fold itself. They have taken seriously the question of personal salvation *within* a communal context, and in the process have undercut the leading religious-cultural assumptions of their elders.

What is happening then should probably be considered a restructuring rather than a revival of religion. It is the attitudes toward the old values and the old values themselves that have changed. And the institutions which profess the old values, such as the institutionalized churches, have lost their popularity.

The result is that the churches and synagogues, all churches and synagogues, are in trouble. How great is the challenge? Does it render religion obsolete? Has it lessened the need for faith?

Rabbi Alexander M. Schindler, vice president of The Union of American Hebrew Congregations, offers one answer to these questions:

If anything, change has deepened man's need for faith. When a man stands on shifting ground, and whirlwinds rage about, he requires above all bearings, direction, and thrust. He stands in burning need of standards, of values sufficiently enduring to give him a sense of permanence in the midst of seething change. Religion provides precisely such rootage, this needed sense of continuity—not just with its ideas and ideals but with its ritual as well. They give us added anchorage, another means to orient ourselves in space and time. Religion speaks more to the inner than the outer man; and man, in his essential nature, has not changed as has his world. The inner man is still the same. Within that inner world, a thousand years are but as yesterdays when it is past. Man's joys and griefs, his passions and his dreams, these are as they were millennia ago.

CHAPTER TWO

Pointing skyward in a gesture symbolizing the Jesus People's belief that "Christ's Way is the Only Way," the leader of this gathering exhorts onlookers to bury their past lives and devote themselves to Jesus Christ.

The Jesus People

It is four days before Christmas. In a middle-class suburb of Washington, D.C., the windows and doors are decorated with the tinsel and color of the holiday season, and from a building atop a small hill in the neighborhood the melodious refrain of a gospel song can be heard:

> "And they'll know we are
> Christians by our love,
> By our love, Yes,
> they'll know we are
> Christians by our love."

The building is a recreation hall, not a church. It is a Tuesday evening, not a Sunday morning. And the singers, some black, most white, belong to numerous religious denominations. Almost entirely young people between the ages of fourteen and twenty-five, they bow their heads when the singing is over. Then clutching their well-worn copies of the Bible and seated cross-legged on the floor before a crackling fire, they begin, one by one, to speak out in conversational prayer, their heads lowered: "Thank you, Jesus, for being right here in our midst . . . Lord, I thank You for all the love You have showered down on us . . . We are so grateful that You have brought us here together . . ."

They are Jesus People or Jesus Kids or Jesus Freaks (a term many are not very fond of), and they represent, we are told, a spiritual awakening or "revival" that is sweeping America.

The Jesus People movement emerged in 1967, the year of the Haight-Ashbury riots, topless dancers, violent campus demonstrations, peace marches, "Berkeley rebels," Black Panthers, underground newspapers, the soaring use of marijuana and LSD, and the appearance of assorted Eastern gurus.

The roots of the movement go back much farther than 1967, but it was in that year that the Jesus People appeared noticeably on the drug scene and in both Protestant and Catholic Bible study groups. Hippies began reading the Bible in large numbers. Suddenly the Bible was better than drugs. Suddenly it was hip to be holy. It was hip to get high on Jesus. In the Haight-Ashbury section of San Francisco, storefront coffee houses run by concerned ministers began to draw crowds of young Bible readers.

As Archbishop Fulton J. Sheen put it: "When the nuns gave up their long habits, the girls put on maxi coats. When the rosary as a devotion was stopped, the hippies put beads around their necks. When mysticism evaporated into an irrelevant ideal, youth sought ecstasy not through the long haul of asceticism, but through the short trip of pharmaceuticals."

And when the short trip was over, the new "high" of the Bible seemed to last longer. Young people began to hail Jesus Christ as their hero. Today, he is the "in thing," a friend, a star, even a superstar. "I never knew Jesus was so great," is the typical comment of a growing number of young people.

They express their philosophy in "Jesus parties," Jesus records, Jesus posters ("All Power Thru Jesus!"), Jesus decals ("Smile, God Loves You!"), Jesus buttons ("Read Your Bible. It'll Scare the Hell out of You."), Jesus T-shirts, and Jesus bumper stickers ("If You Hear a Trumpet Blast, Grab the Wheel. The Driver has an Appointment to Meet Jesus!").

They rock the buildings in which they hold their meetings with the sound of their Jesus cheer: "Gimme a J! Gimme an E! Gimme an S! Gimme a U! Gimme another S! JESUS! JESUS! JESUS!" There is even a Jesus wristwatch, selling for $19.95 and advertised as containing "an ever-revolving crimson heart to tick off the minutes of the day." Commercial exploitation? Not at all, maintains the publicist for the company making the watch: "The integrity of Jesus is retained. We haven't made a pop head out of him. All we've done is given him a smile. We've taken him out of the church and off the cross and put him on a watch."

The Jesus People movement is nationwide, apolitical, fundamentalist, Bible-oriented, and student-led. At the heart of it is the belief that Christianity should be a personal, spiritual style of life, not just a matter of going to church on Sunday. Jesus, they believe, is more than an idea, he is a presence that can be felt. Many Jesus People object to traditional churches because they feel Christ has been left in the sanctuary. One student expressed the views of many members of the movement when he said, "Jesus is being preached from the pulpit on Sunday morning, but when it comes to interacting with fellow Christians, or any other person for that matter, He is all too often put on the shelf to assume the role of a figurehead.

The Jesus People lack clear definition and numbers. There is no central organization or headquarters, but the movement, which is estimated by traditional church people to total some 300,000 young people, does not lack energy or enthusiasm. As the evangelist Billy Graham put it, "Youth are turning to Christ on a scale that perhaps we've never known in human history."

There are "turned-on-to-Jesus" youths everywhere. They meet nightly in middle-class suburbs all across the country to read their Bibles and "get high on Christ." They congregate along the beaches in Southern California, extending their arms with index fingers pointing heavenward in the Jesus People "only way" sign. They line the cliffs to watch ministers of the Calvary Chapel near Costa Mesa, California, conduct mass baptisms and implore converted hippies to bury their past lives. They meet in an ice cream parlor on a North Carolina beach to hear the gospel preached. And in Santa Barbara, California, the movement has become so popular that the Jesus People have devised a special slogan, "Come to Santa Barbara for sun and Son!"

Caught up in this highly emotional spirit, many younger, high-school-age "Jesus Freaks" have begun to hold Bible studies and prayer meetings in high school cafeterias, schoolyards, gymnasiums, and classrooms—all with the permission of their teachers and principals.

"Why do people call you Jesus Freaks?" the teacher of a Spokane, Washington, student asked openly in an English class. The answer, typical of one all Jesus People might give, was: "Jesus Freaks are people who are freaked out on Jesus. Unlike dope freaks, sex freaks, and materialistic freaks, we found something that's real—Jesus."

A discussion developed, and one student asked, "What about people who go to church on Sunday and then go home and do their own thing? Will they go to Hell?"

The girl who had responded to the first question replied, "Well, if a woman has a husband and only sees him once a week for an hour or two, what kind of a relationship would they have? Jesus wants a true relationship—not a religion."

The questions and answers continued.

Teacher: "How do you go about getting Jesus?"

Student: "By believing that Jesus died for your sins, asking Him to forgive you and letting Him take over your life so you can do His will. He'll give you a new life."

Teacher: "Why have you given your life for Jesus?"

Student: "I had religion for 16 years, and it was a drag. I was tired of telling people I was a Christian when I didn't even know what one was. So I went out into the world and got burnt out on drugs, material things and never finding a dude that loved me. I was living just to live."

Teacher: "How come so many people are 'turning on' to Jesus?"

Student: "Because Jesus is pouring out His Spirit and the gospel is being preached throughout the world. After everyone has heard—then comes the end."

In another high school, in Rosemead, California, a reporter asked these questions in a feature story for her school paper: "How come all of a sudden people are turning on to a man that lived some two thousand years ago? . . . Today in our lives, we definitely need purpose, peace of mind, and most important of all, love and understanding between one another. Is Jesus

Christ, who is becoming more alive to more and more people, the answer to our needs?"

Yes, the Jesus People would emphatically reply, adding that it is their duty to "turn other people on" to Christ. "I am compelled to GO out on the streets and GO everyplace where people are to tell you that God has sent me with the good news that He lives and Jesus said to tell you that he still loves you too," is the way one Jesus newspaper *The Truth* described the Jesus People's commitment to evangelism.

Street evangelism is one of the basic means by which Jesus People spread God's word. In Toronto, Canada, a thirty-nine-year-old street evangelist gave this lecture to a group of Jesus People. Throughout his talk, there were murmurs of "Amen" and "Yes Lord":

> Once a crowd gathers or interest is shown we stop and tell what Christ has done for us. We don't shout that they're all sinners going to hell or condemn anybody; our message is simple—Jesus loves you. He's worked miracles in our lives and given us freedom. He can do it for you. We have to be positive, man. The world is dying for lack of love. People are depressed and sad. Tell them about the joy and peace that you have found yourself. To do this you have to be real and you have to know Jesus personally. I wanted deliverance from bondage myself and so do they.
>
> You have to live Christianity. It's not out there somewhere. It's right here between people. The spirit of religion is the most deadly thing in the world today. It makes you go to church, to Bible study and all that, in a formal way, and people grow spiritually fat. If you want to be a free cat you need vitamins, minerals and training. That is, you need to be told the truth; you need to be completely real with others. What many religious people practice is manners and phony politeness instead of love. How can we do this and still say God's Spirit is a Spirit of truth?

After his talk, there was a prayer meeting, and then the Jesus people went out into the streets to preach the message they had just heard.

Another topic that is discussed wherever Jesus People meet is the drug issue or, more specifically, their rejection of drugs.

The publisher of an underground Jesus People newspaper displays posters used by street evangelists to attract the attention of passers-by.

Mrs. Lydia Little, leader of the Christian fellowship TAG (Take and Give) group described at the beginning of this chapter, estimates that about 30 percent of the young people who attend meetings at the recreation hall have been exposed to drugs at one time or another and are now going "straight"; this, she says, is probably far below the percentage of ex-do-pers who have embraced the movement.

Another interested observer, Professor Robert S. Ellwood, a teacher of religion at the University of California, believes youth are rejecting both drugs and Eastern mysticism. Young Americans, he says, are turning away from "the configuration of symbols and gods in the 'head mysticism' of the 1960s and are focusing on one man—Jesus. They feel they are reaching the same kind of infinity consciousness—but without drugs or meditation."

To spread their pro-Christ, extremely strong anti-drug message, the Jesus People have turned to the press—their *own* press. There are approximately fifty-five Jesus newspapers in the United States. There is also a Jesus News Service International, which keeps each paper informed about events taking place in other parts of the country.

The Jesus papers are staffed largely by volunteer helpers instead of professional writers, and most are published monthly. In hip language, they describe Jesus as the "ultimate trip" and the "greatest high." Instead of the features on sex, drugs, and anarchy that characterized the underground press of the pre-Jesus movement, the emphasis today is almost entirely on the theme, "Jesus Loves You."

There is also frequent discussion about the nature of religious commitment. Many Jesus People are dissatisfied with conventional religious services and the existing church structure. Thus, although lay leaders of the Jesus People encourage members to attend conventional churches, the movement is flourishing for the most part outside of the organized church. As one young worshipper said joyfully after the TAG meeting, her eyes sparkling and a smile lighting her face: "Did you see us? Did you see how we raised our hands and touched each other? We could not do that in our own churches."

Another young student expressed it more bluntly in a letter to a Lutheran youth tabloid, *Speak Out*:

> Many churches have not been concerned with people and salvation, but rather with the church building and things. Thus, they have not loved, prayed for, or gotten involved with their young people. I mean involvement beyond just providing a place for the League to meet and some funds for their activities. I see the lack of personal communication centered around and in Christ Jesus.

A similar disavowal of the methods of the established church appeared in the country's largest Jesus newspaper, the *Hollywood Free Press*:

> It's just about impossible to function in today's world and not feel the presence of man's social hysteria. Man is not at peace with himself or with the complex world he lives in. He is uptight about the present and threatened by the future and it's pretty obvious that he's searching for a WAY OUT. It's one thing to rap about the ecological crisis, racial hatred, international conflicts, and our "lost generation" of young drop-outs. It's quite another thing to have a mature understanding of these issues and to comprehend what the solution really is—a real solution that gives satisfying answers and not just a cop-out social prescription.
>
> In the middle of all this confusion, there is one Man who has the apparent audacity to claim that He knows how to get it together. Without apology, He offers no formulas or self-improvement instructions. He rejects every form of religious gimmickry and makes it quite clear that trying to make a good impression is not where it's at. . . . Not by coincidence, this Man just happens to be Jesus of Nazareth.

On and on it goes, the testimony from hundreds, from thousands of "turned-on-to-Christ" youngsters, all expressing dissatisfaction with the way things are or with the way things have been. "These kids hate impersonalness, bigness, irrelevance, materialism—and I've just given you a description of the average institutional church," said one of the directors of a Bible-teaching group called the Jesus Christ Light and Power Company, which operates from an old fraternity house on the University of California at Los Angeles campus and claims to

A young man belonging to the ascetic Children of God group meditates in a Washington, D.C. coffee house. Members of this sect dress in sackcloth to demonstrate their commitment to Jesus Christ and their renunciation of worldly goods.

have reached thousands of these youths. "The kids are tired of hearing about raising the building fund as a 'challenge to faith.' Young people are extremely simple and honest about their approach to the scriptures."

Many of the organized churches realize this and are actively helping the Jesus People movement. For example, the Hollywood First Presbyterian Church is sponsoring a youth-oriented coffee house called The Salt Company which performs Jesus folk and rock concerts twice a week. And in the affluent commuter town of Chappaqua, New York, a bearded, twenty-nine-year-old Presbyterian minister turns his ochre-colored church into The New Slant coffee house on weekdays and Saturdays. The coffee house has been a great success, attracting on the average about 200 teenagers each night.

"They feel they can come to me and bad-mouth their own Church experiences," the minister has said. "I make it a point to encourage them to learn what they can of the things they can appreciate in their own Church." The youths who come to the church-turned-coffee house are predominantly Protestants and Catholics, and many of the Catholics appear to be disillusioned with Mass. "First, they have to go," says the minister. "Second, it seems so remote, ritualized and unresponsive to them. I am more concerned with the hearts and minds of these youngsters than with the name on the door of the church where they were baptized. When we get together and agree on our purpose in Christ, those differences are not so big anymore. Kids are turned off by church and adults are uptight about kids and there is a great deal of room in the middle . . . to work with the two groups."

In addition to Christian coffee houses, and at least one "luncheonette ministry" in Newark, New Jersey, which dishes out hot dogs and the Gospel, there are now a number of "Christian night clubs." One of these is run by the Southern Baptist street evangelist Arthur Blessitt, the self-styled "Minister of Sunset Strip" who once chained himself to a cross on the Strip and stayed there for twenty-eight days and who later, with three companions, wheeled and carried a 1,000-pound cross across the country to demonstrate and dramatize his faith.

There is a peace symbol with a cross on top of the door of Blessitt's "His Place," and those who enter are stamped on the hand, as in any other night club. Only the stamp at His Place says "Jesus Loves You."

Blessitt's "His Place" mixes midnight sermons, free coffee, sandwiches, and drug counseling with the "live Christian entertainment" of rock, folk, and soul music. Like most of the Jesus People, the thirty-two-year old Blessit speaks in the language of the young. He also believes in taking the gospel where the action is; he has witnessed on sidewalks, meeting drug addicts, prostitutes, dope pushers, motorcycle gangs, and disenchanted youths in general—all the time preaching the Jesus movement message: "Let Jesus come into your life!"

Many of the young people who have turned on to Christ believe Jesus can come into their lives only if they spend all their time practicing His teachings. For many, this has meant joining a commune. Today, there are an estimated seventy-five Jesus People colonies in America and other parts of the world; all are based on the belief that Christians should live together and share both their material and spiritual wealth. Most feel that their communes are different from those of the "pre-Jesus" sixties. As one member of a West Coast Christian "family" observed: "Hippie communes fall apart because each person is doing his 'own thing.' But a Christian commune grows and thrives because we're all bound together by Jesus."

In the communes, members share meals, chores, and Bible study. Girls do not enter boys' rooms except to clean them. Members learn to accept themselves and each other. The emphasis is on cooperation rather than rules, and the "direction" of Jesus is followed in all matters.

According to Jim Miller, one of fourteen young people who eat and pray together in a Washington, D.C., Christian commune called the Agapé (the Greek word for love) Family, "You get to understand yourself and people better. Basically, we are just people living and working and meeting together in Jesus Christ."

In some cases whole families have joined communes. Near the University of Minnesota campus in Minneapolis, for instance, five families and an unmarried woman joined a com-mune started by the campus minister, United Methodist cler-gyman Robert Ouradnik. "We had to learn to communicate on a meaningful, non-superficial basis," he said. "We didn't realize how little we knew about that at first. But our ability to communicate grew. And that's the biggest plus."

As for the eleven children of the families who shared the three-story home, a former fraternity house, the Rev. Mr. Ouradnik said, "People who knew them before and see them now tell us they seem more stable, more poised and happier."

Like most Christian communes, the Minnesota group pooled its money to take care of rent, food, and utilities. Different teams would do the cooking, the dishes, and the cleaning for a week; then the members of the teams were changed. The adults had private sleeping quarters, and the children were di-vided according to age. The three pre-school boys shared one bedroom; the five grade-schoolers shared the third floor, with movable partitions for boys and girls; and the three high school students each had separate rooms.

The whole experience, said the Rev. Mr. Ouradnik, had been "most meaningful."

Most of the Christian communes are fairly small. One ex-ception is a 1,400-acre farm-commune known as Koinonia (the Greek word for "fellowship"). Twenty-eight adults and twen-ty-four children share this farm in southwest Georgia, doing what one of the group's leaders calls "the same kind of work Jesus Christ did when he was on earth."

The man who made that statement is Millard Fuller, a thir-ty-seven-year-old Alabaman who earned and gave away $1 million before deciding to settle on the farm and "preach, teach and apply the Gospel of Jesus Christ." Another thirty-seven-year-old member, Ladon Sheats, had been earning $40,000 a year as an executive of a computer corporation. He says he has never regretted his decision. "My old life is like a book I've read and finished." These men feel they have aban-doned the hectic chase after money and prestige to become "partners" in the deeper "security" of Christ.

As another member, Bill Londeree, put it, "When you look

back now, you wonder why it was so hard to make this decision in the first place. The security we have is so much greater than you get with monetary means." His wife Peggy added: "I was dead set against it. The whole idea of giving up our money and not being independent any longer was hard to take. For one thing, it meant moving from a fourteen-room house to four rooms. Now my whole set of values has changed. My main value used to be shopping sprees to buy stuff for myself. Here the motivating value is what you can do for other people."

The partners at Koinonia build ranch-style houses and sell them to poor black families for a token $25 to $35 a month, help impoverished farmers get started in business, and find jobs for sharecroppers. The farm was founded in 1942 by the late Baptist preacher Clarence Jordan. It has survived the hostility of unfriendly neighbors, and today has a national following of well-wishers.

Perhaps the most controversial of all the Jesus People groups are the Children of God. Unlike the main body of Jesus People, the Children of God do not believe in taking jobs. Seeking to devote themselves "100 per cent to the Lord," they depend on donations or on the savings of members to run their communes or "colonies." They pass the time attending Bible classes, singing religious songs, doing missionary work, or performing assigned tasks for their households, tasks such as carpentry, housecleaning, or cooking. Each member of this ultra-conservative sect carries a Bible with him at all times, and each can quote Scriptural passages indicating, they maintain, that in twenty years the world will end.

Wearing red sackcloths and carrying wooden staffs, they stand perfectly silent at public meetings to demonstrate their commitment. Occasionally, they lift their voices in a call for repentance.

Like the main body of Jesus People, the Children of God forbid the use of drugs and do not allow sex before marriage.

There are Jesus People communes in other parts of the world as well. In Kabul, Afghanistan, for instance, a group of Jesus People took over the top two floors of a small hotel in the center of the city in order to try to help stranded persons,

37

Members of a Taos, New Mexico, religious commune meet to partake of their evening meal.

particularly those youths who were lured there by the mystery of the religions of the East and were searching, possibly through drugs, to find themselves. The Jesus People named the top floor of the hotel "The Way Out" and began serving free tea—and sympathy—to anyone who wanted it. Rooms on the next to the top floor were made available for as low as twelve cents a night—for a space on the floor.

"This was an experiment," said one member of the organizing team, "but it has proved so successful that we are going to set up similar places wherever the Freaks are gathering—Katmandu, Benares, Goa—wherever we are needed."

In Essen, West Germany, there is a Children of God commune. Its twenty-five members live in a former school building; in the evenings they hold prayer meetings and Bible reading study groups for interested youths.

"When someone comes into the family, it's like starting a new life," says leader Robert Stevens who has adopted the Biblical name of Elisha. At one time he had been on hallucinatory drugs and marijuana; he came to the movement looking for ways to understand himself.

"I tried to find answers in my life," he said. "I just came up with more questions. I met a couple of people on the street. They told me about Jesus. I prayed with them right there on the street. I wasn't strung out (on drugs). Some of the others were, but they have been delivered. We saw people here being delivered from heroin addiction just like that." As he spoke he snapped his fingers.

It is noteworthy, in America especially, that wherever Jesus People gather, there is music, be it the soft strain of a guitar to accompany the singing of a quiet gospel song or the loud rock sound of such pop gospel tunes as "Put Your Hand in the Hand," "Jesus is Just All Right," and "I Guess the Lord Must Be In New York City." The J.C. Power Outlet and The Love Song are two of the new "Jesus rock" musical groups involved in the marriage of religion and entertainment. The drug and sex themes of the sixties are gone, says both *Billboard* and *Variety,* and religion, especially in the form of songs about Jesus, is in as the main theme of popular music.

Jesus Christ Superstar, for instance, came into the theater on the crest of the Jesus People movement; based on Christ's last few days and with its hip Jesus, it is a kind of irreverent reverence. But the success of *Superstar* may be incongruous with the movement.

When the two Britons who wrote the opera, composer Andrew Lloyd Webber and librettist Tim Rice, sat down to put it together, they did so because they were writers, not because they were evangelists. Neither did they write it because of the Jesus People, although they did want to set down this generation's questions about Jesus in the idiom of today's youth. "Christ was just the best story, by far the most inspiring story of the many possibilities we considered," Rice explained.

A New Jersey Jesus People newspaper called *The Ichthus* reflected on the real reason for the show's success:

> It almost freaks you out to see how this musical about Jesus Christ is so popular in a society that generally rejects God and the basics of Christianity. A lot of people say that the reason for its popularity is because it's "in" to get into Jesus. But is this the real reason? Probably the number one reason for its popularity is the fact that middle class America likes it. They like it because it puts Christ in their terms. They like it because it portrays Christ the way they want to see Him. They like it because they finally see Christ as something they can grasp by themselves.

Just as timely as *Superstar* is *Godspell,* a musical celebration of St Matthew's Gospel which uses rock, soft shoe, and lyrical folk tunes to spread the gospel's words. The cast sings, dances and clowns its way through the show. *Godspell,* wrote one critic, "has the power of the strongest straight-laced sermon; it is not necessary to 'sugarcoat' the gospels to make them palatable."

Of *Superstar,* Father Sebastian Moore, a Benedictine scholar, made this interesting observation: "The fact that in the opera they ask not only 'who Jesus is' but 'who does He think He is' is significant because it is central to the Gospel. It is this question that the scribes and pharisees and His enemies are constantly asking Jesus. It is the question which brings up the whole mystery of Christ. The whole theological spin-off comes from that question."

And what is happening with the Gospels is the best example of the "revolutionary" quality of today's turmoil, says Finley P. Dunne, Jr., executive director of the Temple for Understanding in Washington, D.C., an educational organization which seeks to foster improved communication and understanding among the world's major religions. The changes with the Gospels go far beyond the new and livelier translations, he says. "The Gospels are now being thoroughly demythologized, and put in their proper perspective as accounts written a couple of generations after the Crucifixion by deeply concerned people each of whom had a peculiarly local view of the mission of the church. The fact that Paul and James wrestled over the Jewish or Greek nature of the church is commonly recognized, but that those struggles are reflected in the editorial attitudes of the Gospels is only reluctantly admitted."

The point is, he says, that Christians must release themselves from the limited human and social views of the Gospels and find an applicability of the spirit of Jesus to the world in which they live. That would be truly revolutionary.

Is the Jesus People movement itself "revolutionary"? Are the reform movements from within Christianity occurring because of the challenges from without?

Yes and no, says Mr. Dunne. Christianity, he notes, has always had its breakaway groups, groups which may or may not return to the fold after having made their contribution:

> In America this has been particularly true: the new little Baptist churches that sat on the fringes of Colonial life while the Congregational church commanded the green were perhaps indicative of what would continue to happen here. And the peculiarly Christian reform movements that are now in evidence, particularly the desire to break down the walls of the churches and experience the God who dwells in the midst of secular life—should not be interpreted as any desperate search for members or as a sudden spiritual reaction against the technological world.
>
> It represents, rather, a sincere attempt of an established religion within a culture to meet the needs of the people. It is

indeed revolutionary, in that many cherished aspects of the religion are being thrown out the window, but it is typical of Christianity to impel revolutions.

According to Dunne, inspirational religion is fine for "a prophet here or there who can stand the intensity of God's indwelling." But for the average person it doesn't work as a guide to life because Christianity, although originally preached to the sick and the outcast, has become a community religion for people who work hard at their respective trades and endure the harsh realities of life. "The Jesus People will not become true Christians or make a contribution to Christianity until they understand the Crucifixion," says Dunne. "Sacrifice is, at present, the last thing on these people's minds."

There are many other criticisms of the movement. Some Christians, for example, feel that the Jesus People are too aggressive in their street evangelism and too anti-intellectual, simplistic, and emotional in their approach.

Some Jesus People practice demon exorcism and "glossolalia"—speaking in tongues. Many critics claim they have adopted this practice to avoid actual confrontations with real social issues. Thus, the Freaks, it is said, are "freaking" out of life and its real problems into a transcendental escape route.

The magazine *Transaction Society,* which sent interviewers out to get reactions about Jesus People, quoted one liberal, establishment campus minister as saying:

> I think the kind of world in which we live leads to some kind of escape. And some of the same kids who were escaping through heroin are now mainlining Jesus, and confusing Jesus with a way of withdrawing from the world and its problems. I can sympathize with them. There are times when I would like to withdraw too.
>
> Jesus to them is a kind of spirit that they have a union with. Whereas Jesus, for the early Christians, was a man of flesh and blood who took history seriously, and whose concern (was) about the whole man, not just his spirit, not just his soul. Jesus will push someone back into those problems, back into the world, only if they stay with him.

Other critics maintain that the Jesus Movement label was created by the media to grab headlines, that the Jesus People are confused, and that it is not enough merely to understand the philosophy of salvation as expressed in the Bible. Many claim that the unquestioning fundamentalism of the Jesus People is at odds with the best of Biblical allegiance and scholarship; some scholars say it denies the true nature of God's revelation through the Bible, which is contradictory and individualistic.

Some critics are bitter. A girl who spent three months living in various Jesus People communes in order to gather information for her master's thesis in anthropology, complained:

> They are intolerant, incapable of accepting someone who has a modified version of what they believe, someone who refuses to go into a mass ecstasy. . . . Either you pray with them, talk with them, or you are not "saved." There is an exclusivity about this movement. It is not enough to be a Christian. One has to be a spirit-filled Christian. Someone who has any amount of doubt is crucified. They have the whole script rehearsed. They hit you. You were constantly being grilled and they always were prone to judge you.

Other critics are distressed by the direction the Jesus People movement is taking. Radical educator and long-time student of the young, Peter Marin, visited a weekly prayer meeting and found the atmosphere "so antiseptic, so hygienic, so humorless, so innocent and distressing at the same time—a roomful of shiny pennies stamped with the same date." In a *Saturday Review* article, he wrote, "one can hear underneath all the snuffling and scuttling of small animals seeking a place to hide. There is a kind of nostalgia to the meeting, an old-fashioned boosterism and a curious oscillation between zeal and fear. It is as if the last night of summer camp were being held in the hold of the sinking *Titanic*."

So why are the Jesus cults so popular? In Marin's opinion:

> They offer the young what other faiths do not—an instantaneous and push-button forgiveness, an apparent and abrupt end to guilt and self-disgust. They are familial, offer an authoritative Father, brothers, and sisters for company. Though ultimately triumphant, they can explain and justify present

suffering. Though ultimately millennial, they are comfortably regressive, a denial of the probable future and its crises. One becomes a child again. The world is defused, depoliticized. *Jesus is coming*. First the necessary catastrophe, then the New World. There is little one can do save render the State its due and prepare oneself for the Second Coming.

A more optimistic view comes from retired Archbishop Sheen, who believes the rise of the Jesus People should not be attributed to a "belated hero worship of a fellow rebel"—a claim that is sometimes made. Says the Archbishop: "The new youth, unlike the 'old youth' of three years ago, are not looking to Him as a rebel, but as a salvation. The young may be discovering Jesus outside the church, as did their olders, Henri Bergson, Simone Weil and Malcolm Muggeridge."

Another prelate, Bishop Bernard J. Topel of eastern Washington state, often sees things the way the Jesus People do. He raises his own vegetables, cooks his own meals, washes his own clothes, and lives in a modest $4,000 house, paying for all of his living expenses with his $97 monthly Social Security check. He says: "We should question current economic and social standards. I reject them. And I think many of our youth are rejecting them also. The time has come when we should ask ourselves if we Christians have a right— no matter what our wealth—to live in affluence, even in an average way, when others are in need. To do so is certainly not showing the sign of discipleship. It is not proving by our actions the true reality of Christ and His teaching."

Even the pontiff apparently sees some sign of optimism in the Jesus People, noting that "an interest in Christ exists in our modern world, which is so marked by denying or at least forgetting Him."

The evangelist Billy Graham also has spoken out about the Jesus People. The average young person today is "turned off" by the church, he has said; this "whole new generation is frantically searching for the person of Jesus." In some cases the movement is too superficial and too emotional, he concedes, but otherwise he has had nothing but praise for the movement, which he terms a "major spiritual phenomenon."

Addressing the European Congress on Evangelism which met in Amsterdam in 1971, he praised the movement for its Bible-based attitude, its belief in Christ, the Holy Spirit, and the Second Coming of Christ, and its zeal for evangelism and Christian discipleship. Religious conversion has helped many young people get off hard drugs and become more aware of their social responsibilities, says Graham. "All kinds of new social projects are being started by these new Christians. In my own community, where a rather large group of so-called hippies have recently been converted, not only are they spending their time studying the Bible, but they are looking for projects in the community where they can witness by their service."

Has the movement helped bridge the gap between young people and the established church? Dr. Graham for one believes it has: "Many American churches have doubled, and some have tripled their membership and attendance during the past year as a result of this new spiritual movement among young people."

What it all adds up to, says Dr. Gerald Jud, an executive with the Board for Homeland Ministries of the United Church of Christ, is that "young people are finding themselves in a highly-materialistic, success-oriented culture and they are feeling a real longing, a hunger for the sacred, for a sense of transcendence. The organized church . . . is disfunctional in relation to . . . what is happening today. The kids got beat down on such issues as the Vietnam war. They are now very discouraged in relation to injustice, and they are turning in the other direction, some to the Bible."

But, he cautions, the questions raised by the Jesus People are not easily answered. It is a plus that so many youths have become Jesus People, many conventional churchgoers believe. But can they continue to live on the high tide of emotionalism? Will the movement last? Only time will tell.

CHAPTER THREE

Believing himself blessed with the "prayer gift of tongues," this man speaks out in a strange and unknown language; Catholic Pentecostals believe "speaking in tongues" demonstrates their "openness to the power of the Holy Spirit."

Catholic Pentecostals

Fifty days after the crucifixion of Jesus Christ, according to Christian belief, the Holy Ghost descended and gave to the disciples the power of speaking in other than a known human language. The day of Pentecost became a great festival, cele-brated by Christians throughout the world, but the mysterious gift of tongues, today called "glossolalia," was rarely practiced by Christians after 100 A.D.

In modern times, speaking in tongues has been practiced on a small scale, but it has been largely associated with Protestant Pentecostals. Now Roman Catholics are beginning to speak of a new movement in their church, one that is characterized by informal prayer meetings—and this mysterious prayer gift of tongues.

Today there is a growing number of Catholic Pentecostals or Charismatic Catholics in the United States, and the so-called gift of tongues many of them practice is a reflection of the low-key spiritual renewal taking place among America's 48 million Catholics. The number of Catholic Pentecostals is conservatively estimated at 40,000. However, an exact figure is hard to come by since Catholic Pentecostalism is generally an unorganized movement without a strong national structure.

Although church officials do not actively promote Pentecos-talism, many nuns and priests have joined the movement, and they too claim to experience the charismatic gifts of the Holy Ghost at Pentecost. At the Fifth International Conference on the Charismatic Renewal in the Catholic Church, held at South Bend, Indiana, in June 1971, there were some 200 priests and three bishops among the almost 5,000 persons present. And for the 1972 conference, plans have been made to accommodate as many as 10,000 people.

According to Archbishop Philip Hannan of New Orleans this charismatic renewal "is a means of renewing the faith, a means of stimulating prayer, a means of encouraging participation at Mass, a means of uniting Christians in the expression of their beliefs and deep concern for each other."

Accompanying this spirit of renewal is a new air of emotionalism. Catholic Pentecostals generally are not as emotional as Protestant Pentecostals, and leaders of the movement assert that speaking in tongues and other expressions of emotion do not truly characterize the movement as much as the openness of worshippers to "the power of the Spirit" and the "fullness of life in the Holy Spirit." But the emotional aspects do bother some traditional Catholics who refuse to get involved with prayer meetings.

On the other hand, many traditional Catholics are beginning to accept the emotional aspects of Pentecostalism. Auxiliary Bishop Joseph McKinney of Grand Rapids, Michigan, said as much when, while commenting on the Catholic Pentecostal movement, he stated, "A person is considered perfectly normal if he jumps up and down at a football game or if he enjoyed a good party, but if he does this in connection with religion we think he's rather strange. It is my growing conviction that if the life in Christ means so much to people that they are enthusiastic about it and can use their whole being in giving praise to God—emotions and body as well as will and intellect—more power to them."

There are some Protestants in the Catholic Pentecostal movement, but for the most part the members of charismatic renewal are Catholic. Essentially, they believe that speaking in tongues and other gifts of the first Pentecost such as healing and prophecy should be practiced in the church today.

The Holy Spirit, they believe, will manifest Himself in the daily life of the average, sincere Christian. In a typical prayer meeting, at the Catholic University of America in Washington, D.C., there was considerable singing, gesturing, and spontaneous prayer. There were no "rules," only the feeling that all things should be done in the spirit of edification.

This particular meeting began when a young priest wearing slacks and a sports shirt rose to tell the 300 people assembled that "Jesus Christ is in our presence right now, wanting to save us and make us free. The Lord really makes us free by the power of his word, and this Friday night the Lord will speak his word to us in many ways. We have to open ourselves to the saving and freeing power of Jesus Christ."

A girl started strumming a guitar and all began to sing:

The Spirit is a-moving, all over, all over this land.

People are gathering, the Church is born. The Spirit is a-blowing on a world reborn.

Doors are opening as the Spirit comes. His fire is burning in His people now.

Filled with the Spirit, we are sent to serve; we are called out as brothers, we are called to work.

The world born once is born again.
We recreate it in love and joy . . .

During the meeting, people rose to share events which had happened to them during the week. Others spoke out to start songs or prayers or to give some inspired preaching. One worshipper rose to say she had received the gift of tongues.

In similar meetings throughout the country, Catholics gather in private homes or church halls. There is hymn singing, testimonials, fellowship, Bible reading, and sometimes, speaking in tongues. Some of the sessions have been said to evoke the atmosphere of old-fashioned revival meetings. Often shouts of "Thank You, Jesus!" and "Praise the Lord!" mingle with the lively sounds of hand clapping and the music from tambourines and guitars.

The Pentecostals are not long-haired "hippie" types. Unlike the Jesus People and the devotees of the Eastern religions, who

49

are mainly young people, the Pentecostals include people of all ages. But like the other new movements, they do represent a challenge to the great body of traditional Catholics who cling to the "unemotional" religious practices of their faith.

Informal, spontaneous prayer gatherings are not new to the Catholic church. Eucharistic assemblies in the early church exhibited this characteristic. But over the centuries spontaneous individual prayer became silent and public prayers began to follow fixed texts. For hundreds of years it was extremely rare to find Catholics praying together aloud and spontaneously. In modern church history this style of prayer has been a characteristic of Methodists and Quakers.

Catholic Pentecostals have not abandoned the Mass. In fact many Pentecostals maintain that participation in the movement has strengthened their devotion to the Mass. Some features of the Mass, including Scripture reading, public prayer, songs, and thanksgiving, are common to the Pentecostal prayer meetings. But with their emphasis on singing, gestures, praise, and spontaneous prayer, the Pentecostal meetings are vastly different from the principal act of worship in the Catholic Church—the Mass.

No two prayer meetings are ever exactly alike, and today these meetings have become the principal vehicle for the nationwide movement. Pentecostals look upon the meetings as a new way to pray, one that is characterized by the praise of God. As a result, Pentecostalism, or the Charismatic Renewal Movement, as it is more formally called, is said to be giving many Catholics a new life of faith. Kevin Ranaghan, one of the spokesmen for the movement and a member of a Pentecostal group in South Bend, Indiana, says "There are lots of movements in the church which have been pushing in this direction, but I have never known anything in the life of the Catholic church make Catholics draw so close and so deeply to the Bible as . . . this charismatic renewal."

Another observer of the movement, William J. Whalen, testified in U.S. Catholic and Jubilee magazine:

> One thing that struck me in talking with Catholic Pentecostals is that they display what many of their fellow Catholics

seem to lack: conviction and enthusiasm. One after another told me that he was on the verge of losing his faith or had already stopped going to Mass before he found new strength at the prayer meetings. Catholic Pentecostals related that they had memorized catechism lessons for years in parochial schools but had never 'experienced' Jesus Christ or had any real assurance that God was alive. For most of these, the baptism of the Holy Spirit, or whatever anyone wishes to call this spiritual experience, has given new direction and hope. They invariably try to interest their relatives and friends in Pentecostalism, and so the movement grows.

As it grows, so does the controversy surrounding the most talked-about aspect of the movement, the speaking in tongues. Although many Catholics consider this to be the least of the gifts "bestowed" by the Holy Spirit on Pentecost, it never ceases to draw the most attention. A great number of Catholics, like Bishop Joseph Hogan of Rochester, New York, are cautious about this gift. But many also accept, as does he, the need for "the gifts of tongues, prophecy, interpretation and even healing" to be found in Catholic Pentecostal groups. In fact, says this prelate, "I find it a strong and persuasive argument that these gifts are necessary in the neo-pagan age as they were among the early Christians who had to face the paganism of Rome . . . I sincerely believe that the movement offers new hope for a Church whose structures have been mercilessly criticized by its own members."

That the early Christians engaged in glossolalia can be found in St. Paul's instructions to the Corinthians (1 Cor. 14:26-33):

> What then is to be done brethren? When you come together each of you has a hymn, has an instruction, has a revelation, has a tongue, has an interpretation. Let all things be done unto edification. If anyone speaks in a tongue, let it be by twos or at most by threes, and let them speak in turn, and let one interpret. But if there is no interpreter, let him keep silence in the church and speak to himself and to God. Of the prophets, let two or three speak at a meeting, and let the rest act as judges . . . For God is a God of peace, not of disorder.

In the modern age, however, glossolalia has been criticized as being absurd, bizarre, ridiculous, unnecessary, and irrational. By contrast, the Catholic Pentecostal position is that speaking in tongues "is in the nature of a response, a loving response to the wonder and glory of God who in his lavish generosity gives us not only his Son, his love, his life, but even the gift of words with which to thank him."

Glossolalia is not strictly a religious phenomenon. The subject has been treated in books on abnormal psychology, and the relationship between certain personality variables and the practice of speaking in tongues has been studied in a mental health project backed by the National Institutes of Mental Health (NIMH). This study compared 26 "glossolalists" and 13 "nonglossolalists" with tape recordings of glossolalia which had been analyzed. The final progress report of the study noted:

> Linguistic analysis of glossolalia indicates that this speech is not that of an actual language, nor do these utterances have the essential characteristics of any language. The relationship of this phenomenon to hypnotic susceptibility is apparent. Fluid ego controls and flexible regression in a positive transferential relationship permit the person to abandon himself to this babbling with the accompanying feeling of release and acceptance.

Any inferences drawn from this statement should be done so with care. Questioned about glossolalia, a psychologist and chairman of the psychology department of a large university called it a social phenomenon to some extent and said that it is "a little atypical of other dissociative disorders." But he was quick to point out that "the religious angle" is a different matter. It may be that the insights one has while speaking in tongues are "philosophically true," he said. "The psychological motivation for having this experience has nothing to do with the validity of the experience. And just because you can explain the psychological causes of an experience does not mean that the experience itself is a falsehood or is invalid."

It is left then for the speakers of tongues to have the last word. In the book *Catholic Pentecostals*, Kevin and Dorothy Ranaghan observed:

In poetry, music, art, and in so many other ways we try to reach beyond ourselves, to express the inexpressible, to hymn the beauty, the rapture, and even the inevitable ugliness of the world of God's creation. Lovers in the silent depths of wordless glances speak a language only they can hear. In moments, rare moments of intensity "too deep for tears" or too exalted for feeble words, we have known the need, the cry of our beings to create expression, response. If ever words were inadequate it is in the presence of the Word who loves and calls and evokes from us our all. To him be glory and praise forever! . . . This is the *why* of speaking or praying in tongues.

The feeling evoked by speaking in tongues is described in this comment by a girl who believes she has spoken a heavenly language:

There is a certain elation. Our Protestant brethren talk about "release," and I guess that is a pretty good way of saying it. Say you are all tied up in knots about something and you feel you cannot really pray about it. So you just take off in this language and it goes very easily and very quickly. You find that you are making the dispositions of the intentions that you should be making. And then you find that the tongues stop and you feel that the work is done. I have done the job. In English, it would not even go at all. Speaking in tongues leaves you physically refreshed. People are just now discovering that this is possible. Usually in petition praying, for healing, we pray in tongues because our Lord God Holy Spirit, whose language it is, has to know what is going on.

Another controversial practice is the laying on of hands, a prayer gesture that is regarded by some as a sort of pseudo-sacrament and by others as magic and superstition. Pentecostals, however, point to Biblical precedents in the Old and New Testaments for the gesture's use by laymen. They call it a symbol of prayer, analogous to the sign of the cross, or genuflection, and say a layman can do it "in virtue of his being a child of God and a temple of the Holy Spirit."

One leading Pentecostal minister who is critical of all Pentecostal groups who practice the laying on of hands is the Rev. Dr. David Du Plessis of the Apostolic Christian Church. This

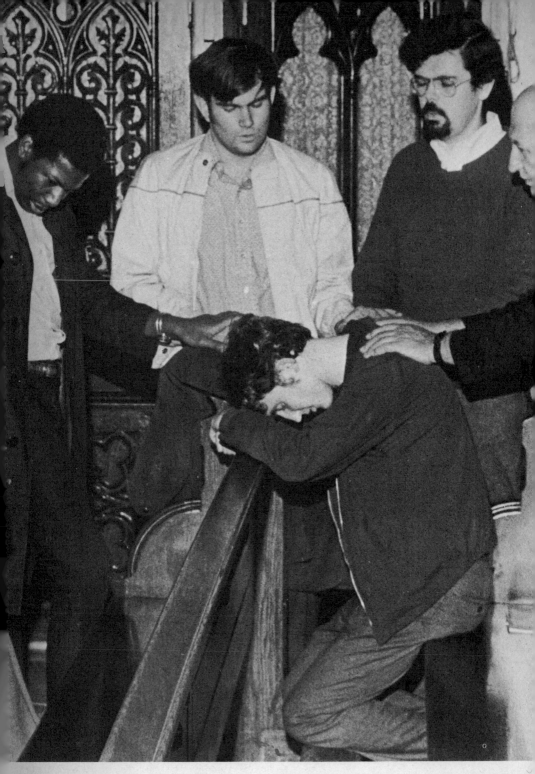

These members of a Catholic Pentecostal group are engaging in the laying on of hands, a controversial practice which they consider to be a prayer gesture similar to the sign of the cross.

globe-trotting clergyman has preached in fifty-two countries and was a guest of the Vatican Secretariat for Christian Unity at the third session of Vatican II. He has ministered in every denomination and has warned one predominantly Catholic Pentecostal gathering against "chaotic carryings-on" at prayer meetings. He notes that in the Bible it says that "at Pentecost the Apostles were seated when they received the spirit—not carrying on like a bunch of holy rollers." As for the laying on of hands, he asserted, "Jesus is the only baptizer. No one gets the baptism from me or from another Pentecostal, but only from Jesus."

Emotionalism that includes shouting, trances, jerking, and hand clapping has long been associated with Protestant Pentecostalism, which includes a great number of revivalist churches, assemblies, and sects. Most have in common a belief in the Trinity, in the virgin birth and deity of Jesus, and in the literal infallibility of the Scriptures. In general, they are also ultrafundamentalistic and work independently of recognized denominational organizations.

Most Protestant Pentecostal sects have either Baptist or Methodist backgrounds. Toward the end of the nineteenth century, for instance, some members of the Methodist Church founded by John Wesley left to start separate Holiness churches, such as the Church of the Nazarene. In 1901 Holiness preacher Charles F. Parham began a Bible school of his own in Topeka, Kansas, and adopted the practice of speaking in tongues as a sign that the baptism of the Holy Spirit had been received by Christians. Parham opened another Bible school in Houston, and a black minister student of his, W. J. Seymour, carried his teachings to Los Angeles where he introduced Pentecostalism to people from all over the country. In that city, in 1906, the "fire of God" is said to have descended on a congregation and to have prompted the establishment of a number of small Pentecostal churches.

There are now an estimated 2 million members of classical Pentecostal churches in the United States; the major ones being the Assemblies of God, the Church of God, Pentecostal Holiness Church, International Church of the Foursquare Gospel, Apostolic Overcoming Holy Church of God, Pentecostal Church of America, and the United Pentecostal Church. Pentecostalism is found in every state in the United States and is particularly strong in the South, West, and Middle West.

Pentecostalism entered a new phase in the 1950s when members of many historical Protestant churches, including some Lutheran, Presbyterian, and Baptist congregations, began to practice the Pentecostal charisms. The members of this new Pentecostal movement, called "Neo-Pentecostalism," generally do not affiliate with Pentecostal churches and have not left the established churches.

The phenomenon within the Catholic church belongs to Neo-Pentecostalism. The highly emotional aspects of classical Pentecostalism have helped to shape the public image of Catholic Pentecostals, but the movement has remained faithful to the traditional Catholic faith. The mere fact, however, that it has appeared within the Catholic church has astounded many observers. Classical Pentecostal bodies have always held that the formalism of Catholicism made it impossible for Catholics to receive the "baptism in the Spirit" without leaving their church. At the same time, the vast majority of Catholics never took the Pentecostals seriously, rejecting the emotionalism of speaking in tongues.

As Father Edward D. O'Connor, C.S.C., has written in *The Pentecostal Movement in the Catholic Church*:

> No one, therefore, was prepared for the ready acceptance which Pentecostal spirituality was to encounter once it had gotten a start in the Catholic Church. It has spread far more rapidly there than in any of the other established churches, and the opposition to it has been much less intransigent. Several Pentecostal observers have commented with surprise on how easily Catholics seem to receive the "baptism in the Spirit." The Catholic hierarchy have been more open and favorable to the movement than the officials of any other church.

The phenomenon first took roots among Catholics at Duquesne University in Pittsburgh in 1967. It then moved on to Notre Dame and Newman Centers at the University of Mich-

The informal prayer meetings of the Catholic Pentecostals are characterized by singing, spontaneous prayer and praise of God, scripture reading, and sometimes the prayer gift of tongues.

igan and Michigan State before spreading to other parts of the United States and Canada.

According to Father O'Connor, many of the charisms of the primitive church, including the speaking in tongues, suddenly reappeared at a retreat held at Duquesne:

> Quite a number of students and faculty had experienced a powerful renewal of their religious life. Some recovered the faith after having lost it completely. Others who had been lukewarm were led to make Christ the living center of their lives. Many found a new power to communicate to others what Christ meant to them. These things had not come about through the work of some inspiring preacher; in fact, there had been no such person involved. Instead, they seemed to be the work of a direct action of the Holy Spirit.

The story faced skeptical and hostile listeners, but word of the charismatic renewal spread to Notre Dame, where Bible vigils and prayer meetings had been going on since the early 1960s. However, these meetings, which consisted of spontaneous prayer, scripture readings, singing and discussion, lacked the spontaneous, humanistic character of the Pentecostal meetings that began at Duquesne. During the first Pentecostal prayer meeting at Notre Dame, about twenty people, including two priests, crowded into a small living room. About half a dozen persons gathered in a semicircle around a person who was to be prayed over. Father O'Connor has described what happened next:

> They laid their hands on his head, and started to pray, at first in English. After a few moments, one of them began to speak something that sounded very much like Arabic. A moment later, another also went into another tongue, which sounded entirely different. Before long, all of those who were praying over the "candidate" were praying in tongues.
>
> The dissimilarity among the tongues was striking. One of them was very musical, full of l and r sounds, and utterly unlike any of the familiar languages of western European origin. It was noticeable also that whereas the one who spoke "Arabic" did so with an accent that sounded very authentic—coughing up the difficult gutturals with facility (whereas most Americans never do learn, even with years

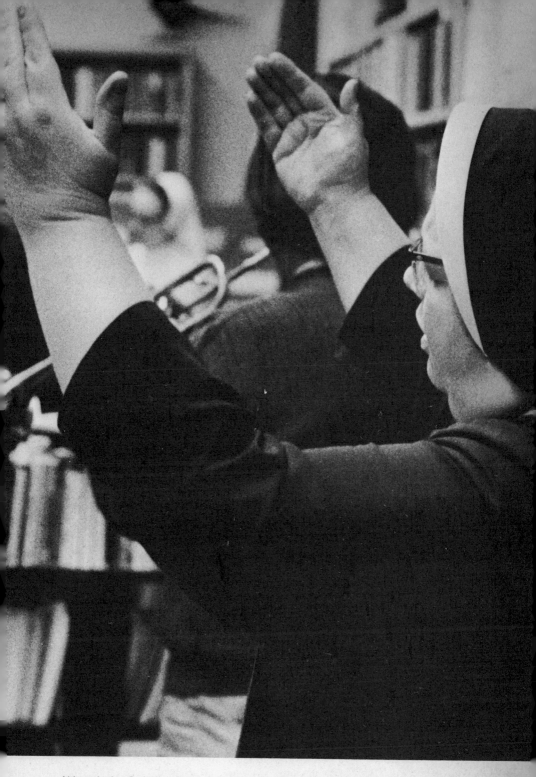

Although the Catholic church has not actively endorsed Pentecostalism, many nuns and priests have joined the movement, and they too claim to experience the charismatic gifts "bestowed" by the Holy Ghost on Pentecost.

of practice, to make correctly these sounds which do not exist in our own language), another spoke his tongue with an accent that was obviously American. However, no one there spoke any language that was understood by anyone else.

There have been countless tongue-speaking sessions since this one. In fact Catholic Pentecostalism has grown so force-fully since 1967 that it is regarded by some observers as one of the most significant modern developments in Christianity. Such praise comes for the most part, however, from advocates of the movement, and even the most enthusiastic admirers will admit that a certain amount of healthy skepticism is in order.

Many admit that there are certain dangers inherent in Pentecostalism. The "gifts" God has conferred may be ex-ploited for the wrong motives. What of the person whose am-bition to be a religious leader is inspired by personal egotism? With his stirring rhetoric, he may simply be experiencing a sense of power in standing before others as God's representa-tive. And what of those who merely love the aura of divine mystery associated with the gifts? Or those who come to the prayer meetings in search of excitement rather than a pure reli-gious experience? What of those who come to satisfy some false spiritual urge? What of those who are excessively emo-tional to begin with and feel themselves encouraged to have il-lusions and hallucinations as a result of emotional prayer meet-ings? These are some of the questions serious Pentecostals are asking themselves.

In 1969 the U.S. Catholic Bishops appointed Bishop Alex-ander M. Zaleski of Lansing, Michigan, to head a commission to study Catholic Pentecostalism. The commission did not draw any definitive conclusions regarding the phenomenon, but it did go on record as saying that the movement should not be inhibited.

The commission report said in part:

> It must be admitted that theologically the movement has le-gitimate reasons for existence. It has a strong biblical basis. It would be difficult to inhibit the working of the Spirit which manifested itself so abundantly in the early Church. The

participants in the Catholic Pentecostal movement claim that they receive certain charismatic gifts. Admittedly, there have been abuses, but the cure is not a denial of their existence but their proper use. We still need further research on the matter of charismatic gifts.

Pentecostalism in the Catholic church is still a relatively new phenomenon and a serious study of the movement's true meaning may be years away. On the other hand, Pentecostalism does represent a challenge to tradition. The Pentecostals are new apostles of a deep desire among people, a religious stirring affecting nearly every Christian denomination.

CHAPTER FOUR

A devotee of Lord Krishna meditates, seemingly oblivious to his surroundings, while a fellow disciple chants the Hindu *mantra: Hare Krishna Hare Krishna Hare Rama Rama Rama.*

The Eastern Religions

They can be seen on New York's Fifth Avenue or on Los Angeles' Wilshire Boulevard or on the streets of dozens of other cities in the United States. And once seen, the devotees of Hare Krishna are not easily forgotten. Wearing saffron and yellow robes, their foreheads marked with white *talik* (clay), the heads of the men shaven except for a pigtail (so that the "Lord Krishna can pull you up to the spiritual sky"), they roam the streets shaking their tambourines and swaying to the rhythm of sing-song chanting.

Enter a Krishna temple, which more likely than not will be a house converted into a temple, and the air will be filled with incense and the sound of Sanscrit chanting. The voices intoning the Hindu *mantra* will be loud and fervent: *Hare Krishna Hare Krishna Krishna Krishna Hare Hare Hare Rama Hare Rama Rama Rama Hare Hare!*

The movement's philosophy is deceptively simple. "Oh, Krishna, please engage me in your service," they chant, Krishna and Rama being names of God, "the supreme absolute truth."

"Hare Krishna is more a science of God culture than a religion," explains a devotee to some people sitting barefoot and cross-legged on the floor of the temple during a weekly *kirtan*, or Sunday service. "Krishna is the name of the supreme being, and chanting is our way of making a link with the supreme to cleanse one's heart so that one can come to peace with himself.

63

It is not necessary to wear robes or to cut one's hair to begin to experience this higher consciousness, this bliss. We are all looking for bliss, but not too many experience it."

Then the curtains are drawn, and the group moves into the main room, which has walls painted yellow and trimmed with pink and gold. There is more chanting, to the beat of a long drum, and while photographs and paintings of His Divine Grace A. C. Bhaktivedanta Swami Prabhupada, spiritual master of the International Society for Krishna Consciousness, gaze benignly at the people assembled, there is more explanation of what has become probably the best known and most visible Eastern religious influence in America:

> Krishna Consciousness is a means to be conscious of your real identity. It is a process of devotional service. Generally, people take up religion for themselves—if they go to heaven it is for them. But Krishna Consciousness is based on pure devotional service to God which means nothing for me but simply to surrender to God and therefore, since God includes everything, what we are surrending to is complete, not just one aspect of life. Krishna Consciousness says that everything should be "God-centered," be it economics, or politics, or eating or whatever. His Divine Grace was born in Bombay some seventy-six years ago into a family of devotees, people who did not care about self-gratification and achieving business position and social status but instead in pleasing Krishna, in finding real bliss, which is not something temporary but eternal.

The disciple explains how in September, 1965, the Swami felt the call to come to the United States. He settled in a suburb of Pittsburgh, then in a loft in New York's Chinatown, and finally in a Second Avenue storefront as gradually his followers grew. Today there are temples in large cities across the United States and a total of about seventy-five around the world. There are about 3,000 full-time initiated devotees and an uncounted number of other followers in the United States.

The devotees of Hare Krishna practice *bahkti* Yoga, eat vegetarian "transcendental food," believe in sex only within marriage, and do not smoke, consume alcohol, or take drugs.

"A devotee is not afraid of dying because the body dies but the person does not," the disciple further explains. "We are conscious of God all the time. We chant. We sing and dance. We eat and there is Krishna philosophy. When we chant with our friends, it is very blissful. You become intoxicated. There is no paranoia."

When asked to explain the Krishna practice of dress, this disciple, named Damodar, replied:

> One of the principles and practices of Yoga is that there are many aids for concentrating on or for serving God, and therefore we have decided to accept this culture whole, complete and as it is, without saying, "Oh well, this is the United States. We should wear suits and ties." We don't say that because we are not concerned whether it is the United States or France or China or whatever. We know everybody is pure spirit soul. We do not care about all these distinctions. We are simply taking culture which is pure and adopting it complete and we are recommending it to others to the extent that if they want to take it up they will be benefited.

At a recent wedding between two converts to Hare Krishna, the bride's father, a Jew, said he did not fully understand Krishna Consciousness: "They are marching to a different drummer. They seem to hear sounds and rhythms that I do not. But it seems to give them a tremendous sense of serenity and spiritual comfort so I do not think we can fault it." The groom's mother, a Catholic, said she did not really understand Krishna Consciousness either. "But if this is what he wants, I am happy because he is happy."

Today young advocates of Eastern teachings can be found everywhere, and he who seeks a new kind of religious experience can choose from a bewildering variety. In what one observer has called "a smorgasbord of cults and creeds, communes and communities," young people by the thousands have turned away from the Judaeo-Christian tradition to embrace the great variety of beliefs contained in such teachings as Krishna Consciousness, Zen Buddhism, Soka Gakkai, Meher Baba, Tibetan Buddhism, Transcendental Meditation, and others.

There seems little doubt that the young who have turned to the East, perhaps in the spirit of the Latin proverb *Ex oriente lux*—"from the East, light," are looking for a fulfillment and a satisfaction that they feel they have not found in religion based on Western ideals. The attraction of the Eastern religions for the Westerner is obvious, says Dr. Winston L. King, Professor of History of Religions at Vanderbilt University in Nashville, Tennessee. As he puts it:

> The largely intellectualized, de-emotionalized religious "worship" of the average ... church, in which any undue bodily activity or emotional expressiveness is rigidly inhibited in the interests of a very quiet and respectable "reverence," seems to be a dried-up vestigial remnant of living religiousness when compared with the Eastern religiosity, which, in all its ranges, from orgiastic rite up to, and including, meditational intensity, is an affair of total existential participation.

Although the Eastern religions are strange to most people they have found a niche in the youth counter-culture. Bookstores are crammed with volumes about them, including do-it-yourself Yoga manuals. Universities are offering new courses in mysticism, Buddhism, Hinduism, and Asian civilizations. There is much talk of *gurus*, or masters, the holy men of the East, and some students have even gone to Asia to study or practice the Eastern religions firsthand.

Why are young people turning to the East? Can the Eastern religions and philosophies make their way in a civilization that is deeply rooted in the Judaeo-Christian tradition? The answers are not easily come by, but it is probably safe to say that young people have turned to the mystic Eastern religions for many of the same reasons that have given rise to the Jesus People movement. Many, for instance, are dissatisfied with the impersonal way religion is practiced in a technological and industrial modern society. But doubts have been raised about the quest for Eastern religiosity. The pursuit of Eastern mysticism, like the pursuit of Jesus, has been called a temporary phenomenon, a fad, a form of escapism, a "cop-out," a reaction against authority and structured religion.

The accusations have some validity, but there also seems to

be some meaning to the Eastern religiosity movement. It does appear to reflect an authentic religious quest for the divine, a real search for religious experience. But very real problems exist for those who attempt to embrace Eastern belief.

To accept the beliefs of the East is not easy. The Westerner must adapt to new techniques and methods. He must adopt a required strict self-discipline and an austere style of living that is quite foreign to him. He must get used to a radical change of life, which in some instances demands withdrawal from the world. Many of the new practitioners find that they must give up material luxuries and renounce their worldly pleasures in order to make "spiritual progress."

What then is the great appeal of Eastern religions? What makes young Americans want to experiment with them? Dr. Winston King has tried to answer this question:

> How easy, how flexible, how infinitely varied, how vast is the universe of religious language in the East! Here specific doctrinal terms are, on the whole, of no great consequence. If one finds one set of terms useless to him religiously, he may choose another more inclusive and "higher" set. For God, or Supreme Reality, has many names in the East, not just one correct one by which all men must be saved. Here, also, one is not confined to a small three-decker universe of a few thousand years' duration; for in Eastern cosmology, there are universes within universes, and their rise, existence, and fall are an eternal process.

For many Americans, their first inkling that young people were turning toward the East came in the late 1960s when the Maharishi ("great sage") Mahesh Yogi reached the height of his popularity in the United States. With his flowing white hair and robes, his gentle looks and air of serenity, and his philosophy of Transcendental Meditation, or "controlled thinking," he attracted a wide group of followers, many of whom had formerly been users of LSD, a drug with the power to undermine a person's emotional stability and to cause acute mental side effects.

Long before the Maharishi came onto the scene, however,

many LSD users had discovered that drugs do not change reality. They had begun to drop out of the drug world and to seek a more "natural high." Many turned to the Eastern disciplines. Yoga, which is the intricate Hindu system of physical and breathing exercises for achieving control over mind and body, attracted thousands of new devotees. Soon many of its most ardent practitioners began turning to other Eastern sects that reject the use of drugs. Most of these groups believe that enlightenment can come only after the individual has mastered the rigorous techniques of meditation.

Thus the stage was set for the Maharishi and his philosophy of Transcendental Meditation. The media turned its spotlight on the "Great Sage," and his advent on the scene was hailed by many as marking the beginning of the post-LSD generation.

To his young American followers, the Maharishi taught that it was man's duty to be happy. If one sat still for only about twenty minutes each day, he said, reciting over and over again a secret word or phrase called a *mantra*, which would be given to the devotee by his *guru*, tension would disappear and happiness descend upon the believer. Transcendental Meditation offers the promise of solving all problems, the Maharishi said and "if the existence of the supreme, almighty, personal God cannot be intellectually conceived, it would appear to be the result of poor understanding" on the part of the individual.

The Beatles and many other artists turned to Transcendental Meditation and claimed that it inspired them in the development of their art by strengthening subtle inner perceptions. The Maharishi explained that to achieve this enlightenment, the individual must turn his "attention inwards towards the subtler levels of a thought until the mind transcends the experience of the subtlest state of the thought and arrives at the source of the thought."

The Maharishi returned to India in 1968, but by that time many had been turned off by his teachings. Although the movement is still very much alive in America, many have given it up because they did not like having to pay to be told their *mantra* or because they were discouraged with the results.

A number of other cults that appeared in the United States

in the sixties also espouse the practice of reciting a *mantra* in order to achieve "peak experience." These groups are still small, and many insist that their beliefs should not be classed as religions but as systems of metaphysical truths which can be used to increase the power of the mind.

Yet most have a great deal in common. As Professor Robert S. Ellwood, an expert on Eastern religions, observed in the magazine, *History of Religions:*

> They focus around a particular, different experience of the sacred; it is found in the ecstatic experience. This experience for them is always set against the background of a temporal and nonhistorical cosmos. And the space intervening between the devotee and the ultimate is always peopled with semidivine helpers—Masters, spirit guides, UFO occupants, revived pagan gods, or the saints, Buddhas, and gods of the East. The Absolute is less personal than for the normative Western tradition; the void between far more so. The spokesman for this new sacred cosmos is not the emissary prophet, acting as by proxy on behalf of God, but the shamanistic ecstatic, subjectively continuous with the sacred. These groups share with Shamanism not only the general typology of the charismatic seer, but to a remarkable extent details of the pattern, including the spirit band, subjective initiation, learned or spontaneous ritual, antihistoricism, the bringing of wisdom from far away geographical or supernatural places, healing power, and above all the teaching of techniques of ecstasy.

Most of the new religions are Asian in origin, and central to the whole movement is the Eastern belief that man can isolate his inner self. Many of the sects also believe that man has an innate divinity. "If we think of God, we become God," the Vedantin Swami Trigunatitananda has said. "It is not by hypnotism, but by thought; not by transfer of thought or materialization, but sheer scientific fact that we can become God."

Thus, as Dr. Frederick Holck, assistant professor and chairman of the departments of philosophy and religion at Cleveland State University, has explained: "Eastern religion implies an optimism and a confidence in human potentiality that are most impressive, especially to the technically oriented

Calm, serene, tranquil is the life of meditation chosen by this Zen Buddhist monk.

man of the West. It promises the successful seeker not only that he will conquer tension, suffering and ignorance, but even that he can overcome the laws of nature."

The seeker tries to attain this through "release from suffering" and the transformation, not the satisfaction, of desires. Most important, he uses practical techniques.

One of the major Eastern religions that strongly puts forth this instrumental aspect of religion is Zen Buddhism. There are Zen centers today in San Francisco, Los Angeles, Los Altos, San Diego, Philadelphia, Rochester, Honolulu, Seattle, New York, and Berkeley, among others, and in these centers it is possible to see the figures of Buddha, to hear the monotonous chanting in Japanese, and to see the devotees waiting for *satori*, the Zen term for a flash of insight into the unity of nature, or a feeling of oneness with all things.

The great popularizer and interpreter of Zen Buddhism in the West was Daisetz T. Suzuki (1870-1966) who came to the United States in the 1890s and introduced Americans to the Buddhist interpretation of man's relation to nature. Suzuki characterized the Western attitude toward nature as leaning toward exploration, analysis, and conquest, with emphasis on the concept of the individual exploiting nature for pleasure or profit, while the Buddhist, he observed, seeks the "oneness" which is so central to the Zen philosophy.

Trying to explain the differences between the two, he noted that a Westerner who climbed a difficult mountain would speak of conquering it, but a Zen Buddhist would say that he had made a friend of it. Entering the Zen outlook is "like stepping through Alice's looking glass," Huston Smith, Professor of Philosophy at the Massachusetts Institute of Technology (MIT), has said. "One finds oneself in a topsy-turvy wonderland in which everything seems quite mad—charmingly mad for the most part but mad all the same. It is a world of bewildering dialogues, obscure conundrums, stunning paradoxes, flagrant contradictions, and abrupt non sequiturs, all carried off in the most urbane, cheerful, and innocent style."

He gives a few examples in his book *The Religions of Man*:

An ancient master, whenever he was asked the meaning of

Zen, lifted one of his fingers. That was his entire answer. Another kicked a ball. Still another slapped the inquirer in the face.

A novice who makes a respectful allusion to the Buddha is ordered to rinse his mouth out and never utter that dirty word again.

Someone claiming to understand Buddhism in its purity writes the following stanza:

> *"The body is the Bodhi-Tree;*
> *The mind is like the mirror bright.*
> *Take heed to keep it always clean,*
> *And let no dust collect upon it."*

In 1936 Alan Watts published *The Spirit of Zen,* which helped to popularize Zen Buddhism in America, as did the writings of the novelist Jack Kerouac in the late 1950s. Watts, pleading for a revival of an appreciation for mysticism in the Christian institution, has written: "A Christianity which is not basically mystical must become either a political ideology or a mindless fundamentalism."

There are many forms of Buddhism other than Zen. There is traditional Buddhism, for example, which rejects the idea that God is an Absolute Being. Traditional Buddhist philosophy is humanistic and antimetaphysical. Believers have faith that man can understand the nature of things without having to turn to an outside power. "Be a lamp unto yourself," goes a common Buddhist refrain. The frequently quoted *Dhammapada* text of traditional Buddhism states:

> All that we are is the result of what we have thought: it is founded on our thoughts, it is made up of our thoughts. If a man speaks or acts with a pure thought, happiness follows him, like a shadow that never leaves him.

In Buddhism, nothing is static, neither people nor objects nor thoughts; all things are relative. Buddhists have great faith in knowledge, teaching that ignorance breeds suffering and that the right kind of knowledge comes not so much from books as from an awareness of the realities of the nature of life.

Another religious movement that has come to the U.S. from Japan is Soka Gakkai or the Value Creation Society. Its members claim it is the only religion that offers the believer absolute happiness and peace in this world instead of the next. All one has to do to attain perfect happiness and material prosperity is to kneel before a small wooden altar, the *Gohonzon* and chant the Daimoku ritual prayer—*Nam myoho renge kyo*— Glory to the Lotus Sutra of the Mystical Law. The *Gohonzon* contains a replica of a thirteenth century Buddhist scroll called the *Dai-Gohonzon*, the original of which is enshrined in a temple at the foot of Mount Fuji in Japan.

Other than this Soka Gakkai has no structured ritual, no strict moral code, no dogmatic doctrines. There is, however, an underlying assumption that true believers will rise above their desires for material gain and seek spiritual happiness instead. Leaders of the movement also expect devotees to look happy at all times and to convince others to join the movement.

Soka Gakkai was founded in Japan in 1837, but it did not gain prominence there until after World War II when its promise of immediate happiness attracted millions of war-weary Japanese. Today nearly a fourth of the Japanese population belongs to the movement, and the sect claims that there are more than 175,000 members in the United States.

Soka Gakkai is affiliated with the Buddhist Nichiren Shoshu sect and the Japanese Komeito political party, but American devotees generally do not come in contact with the Buddhist monks who lead the Japanese faithful and American devotees of the Church of Nichiren Buddhism are anxious to downplay the political aspects of the religion.

Also popular in America today is I Ching, the ancient Chinese *Book of Changes* which is said to be outselling Freud and Darwin. I Ching is a form of spiritual aid rather than a formalized religion. Through its use the individual tries to understand his conscious and subconscious forces.

In one method of practicing I (meaning "change") Ching (meaning "the ways of fabric"), the psychic state of a coin thrower supposedly influences the number of heads and tails that come up on a coin. Six throws of three coins produces a combination of numbers that correspond to one of sixty-four "hexagrams," each consisting of six lines, in the I Ching book. The individual then reads the pertinent selection or hexagram and tries to apply its meaning to himself and his own personal problem, whatever that problem might be.

I Ching dates back to about 1000 B.C. The early Chinese philosophers before Confucius practiced it, and Confucius and his disciples admired it. I Ching has been practiced in Japan, Korea, and Vietnam and flirted with at scattered locations in the United States.

The Meher Baba cult is described in Peter Rowley's book *New Gods in America* as the "most lovable" of the new religions in America. It was founded by Indian-born Merwan Sheriar Irani who proclaimed he was God, the "Highest of the High," the reincarnation of, among others, Krishna, Buddha, Jesus, and Muhammad.

This bizarre Indian mystic, who died in India in 1969 (his followers would say that he merely "dropped the body") at the age of seventy-four, has inspired Baba communities at such distant points as Myrtle Beach, South Carolina; Schenectady, New York; Hampton, Virginia; Chapel Hill, North Carolina; Boston; New York; Atlanta; Miami; Chicago; Minneapolis; Tucson; Denver; and half a dozen cities in California.

The holy man took a vow of silence in 1925 and afterwards communicated only with an alphabet board and hand gestures. He visited the United States many times and in 1952 was injured in an automobile accident in Prague, Oklahoma—after having predicted, many years before, that he would "shed blood on the American soil."

Peter Rowley estimates that the number of Baba followers is now about 7,000, and all apparently believe in the Baba preaching that, "To penetrate into the essence of all being and significance and to release the fragrance of that inner attainment for the guidance and benefit of others, by expressing, in the world of forms, truth, love, purity and beauty—this is the sole game which has any intrinsic and absolute worth. All other happenings, incidents and attainments can, in themselves, have no lasting peace." Members of the Meher Baba cult claim to have one primary aim in life. This is to find the God in themselves by remembering Baba in everything and by attempting to love him. "Everything else that Meher Baba suggested to his followers regarding such things as drugs, sex, marriage, politics, meditation, and so forth is taken as secondary to this effort to love Baba, to surrender to him, and to accept what they know to be his love for them," Jacob Needleman has written.

There are dozens of other new cults and influences being practiced in America. Some of the leading sects include Tibetan Buddhism, composed of a small group of followers of the Lama Tarthang Tulku, and the experience called Subud, which has as its essence a kind of inner awakening which supposedly brings God, or the sources of life, into the soul. There also are numerous mystic Islamic sects; various Hindu and Buddhist societies; the long-established Vedanta Society, which was brought to the United States late in the nineteenth century by Swami Vivekenanda and is believed to be the first of the Eastern religious traditions to penetrate the West; and, of course, hundreds of Yoga organizations.

While religious experience can be found in Yoga, it should be noted that some forms of Yoga provide no underlying spiritual philosophy at all. A busy executive, for example, may practice Yoga simply to rid him of his tensions. As one scholar of Eastern spirituality has described it, Yoga is really "a culture of the spirit without explicitly relating it to God."

There are many different forms of Yoga. Hatha Yoga is the complicated system of physical postures, relaxation and breathing techniques commonly associated with the term *yoga*. Other forms include Karma Yoga (the practice of selfless service), Bhakti Yoga (love, prayer, and devotion), Raja Yoga (meditation and mastery of the mind), and Jnana Yoga (the path of wisdom through self-awareness).

Still another growing movement to come from the East is The Holy Spirit Association for the Unification of World Christianity, which claims a worldwide membership of 750,000 and promises to dissolve the barriers to understanding that separate different religions.

Frowning in fierce concentration, a young American girl (above) practices the Lotus position at New Delhi's International Centre for Yoga. (Below) A group of young people practice breathing exercises under the direction of Yogi Bjahan.

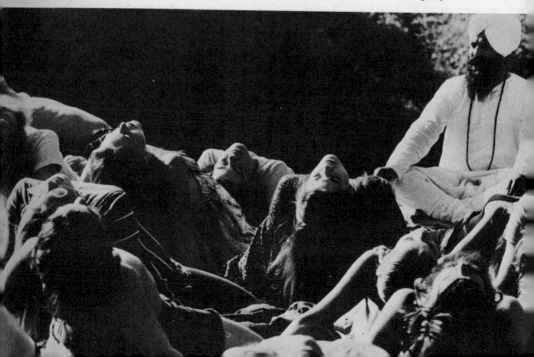

Founded in 1954 in Seoul, South Korea by Myung Moon, the Unification Church hopes to bring together all that is spiritual and "good" in other religions in order to prepare the way for a final age of peace and harmony.

Miss Young Oon Kim, a former professor of the New Testament and comparative religion at Ewha Women's University in Seoul and the church's first missionary to the United States explains the movement's unification philosophy this way:

> All religious philosophies represent different aspects of God's self-revelation to man. Thus, in the past, God revealed Himself somewhat differently to different nations because of cultural, hereditary, and geographical conditions. These differences are now dissolving because of mass communication and high-speed travel. But since all cultures are based only on partial truths, cultural diffusion alone will not restore the world to God. A new universal culture based on a new truth must appear, one which establishes God as the highest value in life. (The Unification Church's) Divine Principle transcends and absorbs these earlier revelations without contradicting their essential doctrines. Rather it explains and resolves their fundamental philosophical problems. We teach that God is absolute and that He created man as a universal being. Whether you are Hindu, Jewish, Christian, Moslem, Buddhist, black, white, or yellow, the essence of your heart is the same and was made to be one with God.

Also central to the teachings of the Unification Church is a strong belief that God intends to establish his kingdom on earth through the propagation of perfect families. According to Dr. Moon, man entered a new age in 1960, an age which will see the Second Coming of Christ. And says Dr. Moon, when Christ comes, he will establish a perfect family that will spread throughout the world by its example of deep family love. One outward expression of this belief was the mass wedding in Seoul in October, 1970, of 777 couples from ten nations. All were members of the Unification Church.

Thus, as Miss Young Oon Kim puts it, the Unification Church has three main goals—"unification of all religions, creation of a world brotherhood of man by establishing God-centered families that transcend all racial, national, and cultural boundaries, and unification of the spiritual and physical worlds centering on perfected man."

The achievement of these goals, says Miss Young Oon Kim, takes constant work:

> Our church motto is "to restore the world, let us go forth with the Father's heart in the shoes of a servant, shedding tears for man, sweat for earth, and blood for heaven." In other words, be a living sacrifice. We are all voluntary, un-paid workers, and everyone is a minister serving others. Most churches focus just on their Sunday services, but we are active all day and week. For this, maturity and team-work is of primary importance. Many of us live in commu-nity centers in order to receive special training, including learning to teach Principle, deepening our spiritual prayer life, basic administration techniques, and anti-Communist theory.

However, she emphasizes, the Unification Church "is not primarily interested in gaining converts, so existing churches need not feel threatened by it. We do not want to steal de-nominational Christians away from their churches; we only want to inform them how to establish an ideal world based upon God's universal principles, thus fulfilling the purpose of both Jesus and Christianity. Even if they accept our teaching, they can stay in their churches if they want."

In *The New Religions,* Jacob Needleman notes that it is not yet possible to evaluate the arrival of the new religions or to judge their influence:

> Ordinarily, we tend to think of the growth of a movement in terms of numbers of adherents. But are we capable of judging between those who merely adopt the terminology of a new teaching without its changing anything essential in their inner lives, and those who are sincerely struggling to live by the teaching? ... Thus, if someone were to predict that in ten or fifty years, twenty million Americans became real Buddhists, that of course would be extraordinary.

College students may be adventurous, but the question re-mains, will they be permanently so? And what about the great mainstream of American life? Many young people "do not understand the tremendous cultural divergence, the inapplicability of many of the Eastern religions to American life," says the Temple of Understanding's F. P. Dunne. "To be a Sikh you really have to be a member of an ethnic group. To be a Hindu of any stripe, you have to abide by religious and social laws that these people would find abhorrent. They may indeed be looking in distant fields for a new religious experience, but they are bound to be disappointed in such exotic models."

Dr. James H. Pyke, Professor of Missions and World Religions at Wesley Theological Seminary in Washington, D.C., puts it this way:

> The Eastern religions have the romantic advantage of being far away, physically and spiritually. They come through a prism of distance and all the more unfortunate and plebian aspects are filtered out. The ordinary Hindu, for example, is still tied to the caste system.
>
> Whether the new beliefs are going to attract more of our young people, I doubt it. There is a strong faddish element in this. I do not mean to imply that there is not a strong commitment. They are sincerely devoted people. But a lot of their challenge is a negative one. They have no connection with the institutional or hierarchical Catholic or Protestant establishment, and it is not so much a positive threat as a negative one in that they are drawing away the young through a seepage rather than through a frontal attack. There is no danger that they will break through the armor of the great religious institutions in this country.
>
> What is different and foreign is attractive. But whether these young people recognize it or not, they are still in the process of finding themselves.

FORTUNE TELLER

Seemingly mesmerized by the flame of her candle, this young "witch" is perhaps trying to summon aid from some dark supernatural power.

The Occult

In 1967, Dr. James A. Pike, Episcopal Bishop of California, astonished church circles by declaring that he had communicated with his dead son, James Jr. A maverick during most of his church life, the prelate developed an intense interest in psychic phenomena and constantly questioned orthodox religious systems. Dr. Pike died in 1969, at the age of fifty-six, after becoming lost on a visit to the Judean wilderness near the Dead Sea. To the Episcopal Church's presiding Bishop, the geographical location of his death symbolized Dr. Pike's "intense desire to get at the source of developments and events for the evidences of the truth in them."

Today it is clear that many people are on the same spiritual odyssey as the controversial theologian from California. The current fashionable interest in the occult may mean different things to different people, but there is little doubt that belief in the supernatural has become a substitute for religious faith for many people.

The young especially are becoming interested in psychic phenomena such as clairvoyance, telepathy, prophecy, and numerology—the use of numbers as symbols for states of consciousness. There are hundreds of "witch covens" (each with 13 witch members) in America today, and courses in parapsychological phenomena are now being offered by dozens of respected educational institutions. In the United States there are more than 10,000 professional astrologers, and tens or perhaps hundreds of thousands of people evince some interest in the subject. Two out of every three daily newspapers in America have astrological columns, some compiled by man, others programmed by computer.

Books on the occult are selling well as youths by the thousands suddenly find great appeal in volumes that promise to reveal "the forbidden secrets of sorcerers, witches, warlocks and satanic rites." Riding particularly high on this new surge of interest in the occult are biographies of the seer and mystic, the late Edgar Cayce who predicted that before the end of the twentieth century California would fall apart and drop into the Pacific Ocean; this prediction received a big boost on February 9, 1971 when an earthquake in Southern California caused more than $400 million in damage. The seer Jeane Dixon also has great influence among large numbers of people. With her often accurate predictions (the deaths of Roosevelt, Gandhi, Marilyn Monroe, and Dag Hammarskjold, among others), she has become something of a legend.

But why include the occult in a book about religion? Should any of it be taken seriously? Is the interest in the occult sciences significant? One serious observer, Father Richard Woods, O. P., believes it is. He thinks the occult "revolution" is a religious response to the impact of technological change and a concrete indictment of contempoary religion. Occultism is to be taken most seriously, he writes in his book *The Occult Revolution*: "For behind its apparent foolishness and surface dangers lies a severe indictment of contemporary society, especially organized religion, science and politics. For many Christians, the occult revolution seriously challenges the life of faith, presenting a novel problem for urban pastors, teachers, worried parents and even the police."

Occultism, he further states, has the power of a "counter-cultural agency," particularly among youth. In their search for meaningful religious experience, many high school and college students are turning away from the churches and synagogues toward the "gnostic climes" of esoteric cults. Thus, Father Woods believes, the quest for the supernatural implied in the occult (the word comes from the Latin, meaning "to cover up or hide") indicates that this new force is a "counter religion."

One of the most popular of the occult sciences is astrology. For many it is just fun, but for countless others astrology sounds a real and comforting note in a world of uncertainty. As Father Woods has written, "Its very persecution by the Church and academy stand astrology in a favorable position for the young critics of the technocratic way of life."

The art of astrology, to give a dictionary definition of the world, is "the study which assumes, and professes to interpret the influence of the heavenly bodies on human affairs." Or, put another way, astrology is the study of planetary cosmic cycles and their relationship to life on earth.

However it may be defined, it is an ancient art. Astrology has been studied by, among others, Egyptians, Persians, Babylonians, Chinese, Indians, and the Chaldeans, who called it the "royal art" because horoscopes were cast primarily for royalty. Ptolemy's *Tetrabiblos,* published in 140 A.D., is the foundation for classical astrology.

Yet despite its popularity and its claim of enabling people to spot certain character traits acquired at birth and thus allow them to better adjust to life, astrology has received little academic acceptance. To most scholars it remains a "pseudo-science" which should be left to the realm of commercialized fortune tellers and the like.

Qualified astrologers who would like to get astrology accepted as a serious science seek to dissociate astrology from fortune-telling, magic, voodooism, and the occult in general. But astrologers themselves sometimes disagree about this. The editor of the astrology magazine *The Aquarian Agent* wrote this answer to a reader who complained about too much occultism in its columns:

> We define astrology as "the study of how the earth interacts with its cosmic environment." As such, astrology applies to all aspects of life on earth, psychology, literature, medicine, philosophy and certainly it is related to graphology, the Tarot, palmistry, I Ching, witchcraft, etc. In addition, in Germany and Austria handwriting is studied with the horoscope to help determine the quality of an individual's re-

sponse to planetary influences; likewise is palmistry studied by Indian astrologers.

However, astrologers hasten to point out, it is important to understand what astrology is really about. Sophisticated astrologers, notes Ralph Metzner in his book *Maps of Consciousness,* "are dealing not with compelling influences, but with tendencies; not with forces, but with inclinations; with *probabilities* to behave, think, feel in certain ways, which the individual could follow or not as he chose." Stated another way, by Dane Rudhyar in *The Practice of Astrology,* "Astrology . . . has no concern with whether a conjunction of planets causes some things to happen to a person or nation; it only indicates the possibility of a certain type of events occurring in a certain place at a certain time."

Thus according to its practitioners astrology offers no "instant high," and newcomers to the field find that their original conceptions of it do not hold up. For example, the celestial signs of the zodiac, which is a map of the earth's yearly cycle around the sun divided into twelve equal parts, can have both positive and negative meanings. Buddha was a Taurus, as was Sigmund Freud and Brahms. But then so was Adolf Hitler. Bernard Baruch, Henry Ford, and Aldous Huxley were born under the sign of Leo. But so was Benito Mussolini. And the different personalities of such public figures as Richard M. Nixon, Fidel Castro, J. Edgar Hoover, Carl Sandburg, Gamal Abdul Nasser, and Albert Schweitzer have all shared the sign of Capricorn.

One of the basic premises of popular astrology is that the twelve signs of the Zodiac have symbolic meanings. If, for instance, you were born when the sun was passing through that part of the great circle in the heavens called Aries, you would be described as having an active and dynamic personality and possess, as one popular astrologer has put it, "natural, charming manners and good mental power; you are fond of having others look up to you." By the same token, if you are a Virgo, astrologers would say you are calm, confident, contented, studious, fond of reading, fact-finding, and possessing an imagination that you use for practical ends. The constellation Libra signifies a personality that is charming, graceful, and pleasing. Beautiful women are supposedly born under this sign and handsome men. Scorpio men, we are told, can attain the necessary self-control for success if they try hard enough. And a "Sagittarius wife," we find out, is a sympathetic listener, a useful helpmate, and a companion in hobbies and sports.

This type of sun sign astrology—there are some 260 different schools of astrology—is generally rejected by serious astrologers, but most will admit that it does serve as an introduction to the realm of supposed planetary influences on our lives. Professional astrologers point out that they need to know not only the date of a person's birth but the precise time and place; even a difference of minutes can have an effect on a reading. Mrs. Jean Byrd, a professional astrologer from Silver Spring, Maryland, tells of having natural childbirth to observe the exact moment of her daughter's birth and noticing later that the doctor's notation on the birth certificate was three minutes off.

"The biggest hang-up about astrology in the modern mind is the junk stuff that is sold over the counter," she says. "Being born under the same sign is absolutely meaningless. Suppose you were born at 9:03 A.M. in New York City on January 13 of a certain year and I was born at Washington, D.C. at the same time and date. Our charts would be different. The planets were not in the same position. When a proper astrology chart is done, it is as unique to you as your own fingerprint. Nobody else has a chart like you."

Regardless of the misconceptions or misinterpretations that astrology has been heir to, it has been receiving wider and wider acceptance. "This is the dawning of the Age of Aquarius," we hear. These lyrics from the musical "Hair" have become something of a national anthem to the pop culture, although many say that the Age of Aquarius will not really "dawn" until 2600 A.D. An "Age" refers to a 2,600 year cycle during which the earth's polar axis changes direction and points to different "pole" stars. We are now in the Piscean Age, which has been closely associated with Christianity because it began around the end of the first century B.C., about the time of the birth of Jesus. Furthermore, the sign of the Fish (Pisces) is also a symbol in the Christian faith.

When the earth's polar axis points toward the star Polaris, the world will enter a new phase called the Aquarian Age. No one knows just when this will happen. It could be 600 years from now, but not since the planet Pluto was discovered in 1939 has a single astrological theme been so popular with the public. If one listens to the music from Hair, one gets the impression that Aquarius will dawn next week or in a few months or few years or perhaps even tomorrow.

The popularity of astrology is only one manifestation of a growing belief, which is particularly prevalent among the young, that the fate of man and the universe is directed by supernatural forces. The fantastic is simply not so fantastic any more. In the preface to *The Morning of the Magicians,* a book that delves into the realms of consciousness, Louis Pauwels writes, "The fantastic is usually thought of as a violation of natural law, as a rising up of the impossible. That is how we conceive it. It is rather a manifestation of natural law, an effect produced by contact with reality—reality perceived directly, not through a filter of habit, prejudice, conformism."

In an attempt to prove that man has more than just a physical body and that there should be deeper understanding of the esoteric arts and sciences, a group of young people founded the free Aquarian University of Maryland which offers such courses as "Cosmic Harmony of Music," "Symbology I," Egyptology, astronomy, Yoga, Unidentified Flying Objects (UFO), and even the Great Seal of the United States, which with its eye, pyramid, and eagle holds a great deal of symbolic interest for some.

The school holds classes in a twenty-seven room mansion in the stately Ruscombe Lane section of Baltimore. It was incorporated at precisely 4:59 P.M. on January 31, 1971, when the position of the stars, astrologers said, pointed to "public education along astrological and spiritual lines."

Most of the students are in their twenties, although some are older, and all apparently have an interest in ceremony and ritual, cosmic harmony, revelations, UFOs, and astrology. A look at the catalog course description for Symbology I, for example, will give an idea of the scope of their esoteric interest:

> Symbology I—The Apocalypse: The interpretation of the symbolic mural "The Apocalypse" and its message for the Aquarian Age. The nature of symbols and their powers. Introduction to the lost continents of Lemuria and Atlantis and the story of their reemergence. Study of the alphabets: Lemurian, Atlantan, Egyptian, Hebrew, Masonic, Latin, Celestial, etc.; numerology and astrological symbolism. The Great Seal of the United States and its meaning for the Aquarian Age. The meaning of the Aquarian Age. The Great Pyramid and its prophecies.

Another branch of the occult which has been attracting numerous followers is witchcraft. To some people witchcraft of all things seems to fulfill their deepest religious needs. Many even claim that witchcraft is an authentic folk religion, a vestige of the nature worship practiced by the pagans in ancient Europe. The British anthropologist Margaret Murray advanced this theory in the 1920's, and many modern "witches" have accepted it, disavowing Satanic or black magic and imitating pagan customs instead. These witches practice what is called white witchcraft. They claim to derive power from the benevolent forces of nature and to use it for healing purposes. One of the most famous of all modern "witches," Sybil Leek, explains that in "pure witchcraft, the life force is all important." Satanism is death, she says, but "*Wicca* (the anglo-saxon term for witchcraft) is a religion designed to preserve life."

With its accent on ceremonial magic, mysticism, and ritualized dancing and singing, witchcraft apparently gives some people a feeling of unity with nature and their fellow human beings. According to Father Woods, "this is (perhaps) the real connection between ancient, medieval, and modern witchcraft—a frustrated longing for natural wholeness and festivity, awesome ceremony, and mystical union with transcendent reality, which is emerging in counter-cultural forms like a rose from thistles—a flower of dark and threatening aspect to the staid and unimaginative weeds."

He further adds, "Whether or not witch covens would be

admitted to the National Council of Churches, and regardless of the truth of claims about continuity with paleolithic worship, contemporary witchcraft is foremost of anything a religion. To be more precise, it is a counter religion or, if you prefer, the religion of a counter culture."

Many witches would agree that witchcraft has become a counter religion. One thirty-two-year-old witch who goes by the name of Cassandra Salem believes some of the interest in witchcraft has arisen because youth are dissatisfied with the established religions. She described witchcraft to a reporter from the *Atlanta Journal* in the following terms:

> Witchcraft is a participatory religion . . . (It) isn't a religion where you go somewhere and sit and listen to a sermon.
>
> This attracts the young person, because he or she is sick of the organized and recognized religions. They want to be active, to take part. Witchcraft offers them just such an opportunity. Witchcraft is actually a return to nature, a worship of the natural gods as opposed to the chrome and glass gods you find in society. We're more interested in finding powers within ourselves, in broadening our own minds. The chants, music, color and things are sort of a way of turning on without drugs. There are among us some who are perfectly good Christians, but they believe this is the way to go because they're disenchanted with the Christian religion. . . . They feel their religion has gotten away from the people.

Black or Satanic magic is as old as civilization itself. The idea behind it is that there are two powerful forces of good and evil constantly at war within man and in the temporal world, each of which can be tapped through the use of ancient rituals and spells. The black witch seeks to put the forces of evil to work to achieve power, success, and material gains.

Some devil worshippers hold similar views. The Church of Satan, which was founded in 1966 by Anton La Vey, for example, holds the view that Satan is the symbol of man's self-gratifying ego. As one of its members put it, "Man, to the Satanist, is an animal but through his own ego and intellect (he) has pulled himself up to the highest level—man is superior and, Satanists believe, . . . should worship his own ego." The

members of this group actively seek material affluence and ad-
vocate indulgence instead of abstinence.

Another group that professes a love for Satan is The Proc-
ess Church of the Final Judgment. Its members say they love
the devil because Christ advised one to love one's enemy.
There are Process chapters throughout the world and in such
American cities as Boston, Chicago, New York, Los Angeles,
San Francisco, Cambridge, Massachusetts; and New Orleans.

The members do *not* worship Satan alone. "We do not dis-
criminate, one may say—that is the key," a Processean
explained. Thus they pray both to Lucifer and to Christ. The
cult is said to resemble the Marcionite ascetic sect that flourished around the first and second centuries. Processeans wear
dark suits "as a symbol of the death of the world" and red Satanic emblems to represent "the blood that man has shed
among his fellow men." Silver in the form of the crosses they
wear supposedly represents "the light of the New Beginning."
Upon the coming of Judgment, they say, "White shall we
wear for the end of the suffering, for the end of pain of countless millions of innocent creatures, whom man has subjugated
and degraded, but whom God shall rise up, and glorify."

Thus Processeans have an optimistic view of the end of the
world. They believe that when it comes, love will reign trium-
phant and repression will be destroyed. The Processeans live in
communes, and the seeming optimism of this philosophy has
drawn new followers to them. Father Woods, for one, notes
that they have a definite "evangelistic tendency" and writes:
"Even in street encounters, the Processeans reveal themselves
to be warmly engaging rather than polemic and dour, and the
fruits of their labors and demeanor is evident in the numbers
of interested young men and women they are attracting."

As an episode of the current interest in the occult, he sees
the Process Church of the Final Judgment as "a happy omen
that a band of religiously committed young men and women
endeavoring to discover value and meaning in a world programmed for self-destruction and courageously proclaiming
their vision of liberation and love can pull it off with grace
and wit in the streets of Babylon."

Why are so many people turning to devil worship and other forms of the occult? According to evangelist Billy Graham, it is because more and more people are turning to Jesus. "The devil," he says, "is also making his pitch." On the other hand, a Canadian theologian, Kenneth Hamilton, puts the blame on demythologized religion, noting that: "Liberal Protestantism excluded anything that could not be explained. But you cannot have religious faith without the existence of a world transcending this one. People are starved of anything transcendent, and they have gone to the oldest and crudest superstitions."

What might the late Bishop Pike have said about the current excursion into the occult? For one who had expressed a belief in an afterlife and the possibility of communication with the dead, it seems fairly safe to say that he would have encouraged it. Spiritualism, like psychiatry and nuclear physics, he said, is one of the new frontiers of knowledge. "Psychiatry was dismissed in this century as nonsense and nuclear physics was considered alchemy when I was in school," he once said.

The prelate resigned from the church in 1969 after asserting that it was a "sick—even dying—institution." He said then, "The poor may inherit the earth, but it would appear that the rich—or at least the rigid, respectable and safe—will inherit the church. Increasingly, the more creative, the more adventurous are out—or stay out; but there are no signs of a mass exodus on the part of the timid and conventional." He spoke of a "credibility gap," a "relevance gap" and a "performance gap" in the church and declared that he had no "believing hope" that the church could adjust itself to modern spiritual needs, which is the same accusation that so many youths are making today.

Before his death Bishop Pike reaffirmed his belief in God and Jesus's Resurrection, but he continued to reject such basic church doctrines as the Trinity and the Virgin Birth. He maintained that fourth century Greek concepts that had lost their meaning were responsible for the Trinity doctrine that says God appeared to man in the three "persons" of Father, Son, and Holy Spirit. "When we say three persons today," he wrote in 1969, "one can't help but think of a committee God.

As to what lies behind this—a living God, whom we relate to and who relates to us in ways that perhaps are described to some degree by these three-fold images—yes, I'm for this."

There is one hypothesis, current today, that general education leads to a decline in supernatural beliefs. But there seems to be no clear-cut proof of this. A preliminary analysis of beliefs in an incoming freshman class at the University of Pennsylvania showed less belief in supernatural phenomena among the more intelligent freshmen. But when supernatural beliefs were separated into "avant-garde" and "traditional," the supposedly more intelligent showed less tendency to decrease their belief in the avant-garde than in the traditional.

"As they move along the academic ladder from undergraduate to graduate studies, students reduce their belief in the unknowable—but not to the vanishing point," observed *The Sciences* magazine, published by the New York Academy of Sciences. "The image of today's young scientist as a coldly rational being is firmly dispelled by earlier studies of male undergraduates in Ghana and at Harvard, and most recently, by an examination of the supernatural beliefs of graduate students."

In the latter study, conducted by University of Pennsylvania psychologist Charles A. Salter and molecular biologist Lewis M. Routledge, ninety-eight male and female graduate students were questioned about "the degree of their belief in astrology, extrasensory perception (ESP), flying saucers, the power of prayer, witchcraft and the existence of an evil force, a supreme being and a personal god."

As the students proceeded with their studies, they showed less of an inclination to believe in the supernatural, but this gradual diminution was slight. To some extent, the degree of belief depended on the area of study. While differences in sex did not appear to matter at all, humanities students had the lowest mean score and the natural and biological science students the lowest score, based on a scale of 0 for complete disbelief in a supernatural force to 20 for unqualified belief. Natural science students expressed almost double the belief in a personal god than liberal arts majors. For the natural scientists belief in witchcraft averaged 5.25 compared to 2.94 for the liberal arts candidates. The average score for belief in an evil force was 4.75 for natural scientists and 3.06 in the liberal arts group, and biologists averaged three points higher than humanities majors in expressing belief in the power of prayer.

The study did not consider social and environmental factors and the researchers came away with no conclusions. But the results made it obvious that today's youth are flirting with supernatural beliefs.

Average Belief by Year of Graduate Study

		1st Year	2nd Year	3rd or More	All Years
1	Astrology	4.37	4.00	3.00	4.16
2	ESP	12.38	12.91	10.00	12.24
3	UFO's	7.31	6.55	5.00	7.14
4	Prayer	7.79	5.64	7.40	7.68
5	Witchcraft	4.19	5.09	2.40	4.12
6	Evil Force	3.61	2.73	2.80	3.40
7	Supreme Being	11.92	12.36	12.00	12.04
8	Personal God	9.95	5.45	8.80	9.56
	Mean	7.69	6.84	6.43	7.54
	No. of Subjects	75	11	10	98

Source: *The Sciences,* Vol. 12, No. 1 Jan.-Feb., 1972.

The new occult interests of today's youth are not confined to astrology, witchcraft, and devil worship. Interest in the mystical is apt to appear with respect to almost anything that appeals to the subconscious mind—there is interest in alchemy, for example, which is concerned with finding an elixir of life from chemical substances, and in the teaching of actualism, which professes that all reality is animate or in motion; man has divine potentials, this doctrine says, and these potentials can be "actualized" in creative expression.

Attempting to foretell the future with Tarot cards has also become popular. These cards supposedly contain a system of symbolic knowledge. The oldest Tarot deck in existence, made for King Charles VI in 1392, is in a Paris museum. But the exact origin of Tarot remains a mystery; some say the Gypsies originated it, others that the cards came from India and were known long before the Gypsies first came to Europe. There is occult symbolism in the Tarot cards, and the one who reads the cards must have mastered this symbolism; he must know the meaning of such typical symbols of the Middle Ages as the High Priestess, the Juggler, the Hermit, the Pope, and the Wheel of Fortune. One hypothetical interpretation of the cards' "magic" is the idea that the shuffler, or inquirer, sub-consciously arranges the cards in a special way.

It would take an encyclopedia to delve into every area of the occult. And then we would probably find that the interest in the occult is not merely an interest in strange phenomena but a symbol of the counter-cultural exploration or response to the demands put upon people by the growth of scientific tech-nology. In many ways it is a challenge to the established church and to institutionalized society.

CHAPTER SIX

Hoping to create an atmosphere of fellowship in which to enjoy their Jewish heritage more fully, these members of the Fabrangen community meet every Friday for an evening meal and religious services.

A Challenge to the Synagogue

The word is *Fabrangen*. Literally translated from Yiddish, it means getting together. But it also means *innovation,* for getting together in the Fabrangen context does not mean meeting at the established synagogue. It means meeting outside of it in order, as a Fabrangen pamphlet puts it, "to bring together the culture, music, customs, language, art, and religion of the Jewish people and make it all more relevant to our existence in America."

Fabrangen, which was founded in 1971 in Washington, D.C., is a community of young Jews, who are trying to rediscover their heritage. For as they put it:

> So much of it has been forgotten and so much of it we never knew existed. Since we were founded, many people have discovered the beauty of our heritage. Poetry, Yiddish, mysticism, legends, dance, prayers, all parts of the identity which we have had to struggle to rediscover. So much of it has been buried. So much has been forgotten.

If this sounds like an indictment of established Judaism, this is probably the case. For the synagogue, like the church, has been called a relic, and the attack on it is coming not only from the young but from some older rabbis as well. The synagogue, these critics say, has not responded to the needs of contemporary society and has not played an effective role in social action.

95

Or so the arguments go. And Jews, young Jews particularly, are challenging, debating, asking questions as they have never asked them before. They want to know: What does it really mean to be Jewish in America? What can they do to express their Jewishness—for Judaism involves religious, cultural, political (in a moral sense), economic, and familial factors. Can there be a Jewish future in America within the "American dream"? Or must it be independent?

Above all, many young Jews want to be relevant, contemporary, and they are expressing themselves in numerous ways to achieve this. There is no single new "movement" within Judaism that reflects this, but there is a clear sense of dissatisfaction among many young Jews who find traditional services unfulfilling, who want a "now" experience, who want to be more "turned on" because they find many of the services spiritually sterile and the synagogue atmosphere bland. They want services that speak to their inner needs, that give them a greater sense of involvement and a feeling of integrity.

Fabrangen is one attempt to give new form to Jewish religious expression. At the Fabrangen Jewish Free Culture Center in Washington, D.C., religious services are held every Friday night. The members, who are mostly in their middle or late twenties, sit in a circle on the floor. Most are casually dressed. In the center of the circle, someone strums a guitar. Everyone joins in the singing, and occasionally someone contributes a prayer or relates an interesting experience. Then they rise, link arms, and dance in a circle to the music of the guitar and the sound of joyful voices singing. "*Shiru La-Adonai Shir Chadash Shiru LaAdonai Kawl Ha-Aretz, Shiru LaAdonai Barchu Shmo,*" they sing. "Sing unto Adonai a new song. Sing unto Adonai all the earth. Sing to Adonai and bless His name."

Afterward the group lights the Sabbath candles, blesses the Sabbath wine, and shares a traditional kosher meal of vegetable curry and brown rice. More prayer follows the meal. This style of worship has become a meaningful way of being Jewish to those who come. As one member put it, "If anyone had told me a year ago that I would be going to Friday night services practically every week of the year, I would have said they were crazy."

The principal founder of Fabrangen is Robert Agus, a young government lawyer and the son of a prominent Baltimore rabbi. Traditional Judaism, he explained, is an "organic culture," a culture in which everything one does is related; there is a purpose behind every action. According to Agus:

> In America this kind of Jewish community has ceased to exist. In the United States Judaism is seen in either one of two ways, either as a religion, which means something that you do once a week or whatever, or as a solely ethnic identification. The religion does not carry over to daily life. Fabrangen has as its purpose to work toward development of a "wholistic" Jewish culture and to give meaning and direction to one's life. In the Judaism that we talk about we mean religious culture and we do not separate religion from secularism.

Fabrangen is trying to span the generation gap in its efforts to make the ancient religion of Judaism more meaningful in the modern world. Many families are involved, and an effort is being made to relate to older people. Some rabbis teach courses at the center, and the Fabrangen members cooperate with a number of synagogues in the Washington, D.C. area. As a result, some of these traditional institutions are moving in the direction of "unstructured" ritual.

Fabrangen remains a local concept, but in cities throughout the United States there are similar groups. Does Fabrangen then represent a discontent with the way things are done in the traditional synagogues? "Yes, I don't think there is any question of that," says Agus. When asked if the Fabrangen "whole culture" concept of Judaism will ever become accepted by Jews in the United States, Agus replied:

> I take what I consider both an optimistic and pessimistic view. I think that ultimately the majority of Jews will continue to exist only marginally as Jews. That is unfortunate but I do not consider it a great tragedy because it has existed for so long. But hopefully more and more sensitive people will adopt new forms—not necessarily what we at

Fabrangen are doing but forms with a similar lifestyle. More and more people will continue to grapple with it, and in the United States as a whole the turn toward organic community, which means community of limited size, will help this movement because Judaism at its best is a great example of organic community.

Outspoken Rabbi Everett Gendler of Lowell, Massachusetts, has suggested that Jews who are looking for an alternative to the synagogue consider sharing their homes for services. In an article for the Jewish journal *Response,* he noted that the traditional synagogue in its present form is an "unlikely agency" for the religious involvement of many of today's concerned Jews. Enlarging upon this theme, he wrote:

> The present synagogue depends on a full-time professional staff whose income needs are constantly rising. The present synagogue also presupposes a sizeable building which, however modest, is still costly to construct, finance, and maintain. . . . Even a slight economic recession threatens its solvency, and it has a built-in tendency . . . to become self-preoccupied, financially and institutionally.

Rabbi Gendler also notes a number of other problems the synagogue must face. He says, for example, that for economic reasons the synagogue must grow in size and that this precludes the kind of intimacy many people are seeking from religious involvement. He also thinks that the structure of the synagogue allows the individual few opportunities "to share his gifts of religious sensibility." In other words, the hierarchical structure of the synagogue prevents the individual from ever leading a service; it keeps him in a "passive relation" to the religious life of the synagogue.

Furthermore, states Rabbi Gendler:

> The religious education which students receive often bears little relation to their homes or lives outside the synagogue. They often find little meaning in the instruction; they retain little; the burden of additional formal class hours added to overly-demanding school days pressures them further, and their indifference to Jewish learning quickly becomes active resistance and hostility.

An atmosphere of lively informality characterizes Fabrangen meetings. Israeli folk songs and dances often follow the religious services.

He also notes that synagogues, like churches, are open to all and that "in their attempts to meet the needs of all in this quite random grouping, there develops a distressing uniformity among the institutions." In other words, according to this argument, if distinctiveness and spontaneity of expression are being sought, the traditional synagogue is not the place for it.

For those who are looking for new ways to express their religious commitment, Rabbi Gendler suggests the following:

> Let us assume that there are three to twelve families in a given area of the city, the suburbs or the countryside who feel that they contain religious, societal, communal interests. These families would arrange to meet on a weekly basis . . . one week a Shabbat evening potluck supper at one home, with the hosts assuming special responsibility for the religious atmosphere, table ceremonies, singing, a home service, etc. . . . Still another week, the groups might meet for a sunset *Havdalah* service with yet a different mood and focus . . . Combined with this would be a program of religious-cultural-social learning centered primarily in the homes and related directly to the weekly coming together of the entire group.

This buildingless synagogue, Rabbi Gendler asserts, would allow people to better share their feelings, problems, and social concerns. A communal lifestyle is one answer, he says, but since most people cannot readily adopt this, there should be an alternative "which could help us grow toward changes in our life styles without demanding, as the starting point, an impossible and immediate break with where we are now."

There is no single movement today that typifies all of the various attempts to rediscover Jewish identity. For example, a number of synagogues and B'nai B'rith Hillel Foundations are attempting to give new form to traditional religious expression by offering folk rock Sabbath services, complete with guitars, soul rock bands, and songs with choruses that go like this:

Come on, people now
　　Smile on your brother
Everybody get together
　　Try to love one another
Right now.

There is also a small but growing number of Jewish groups that are seeking to put Rabbi Gendler's "buildingless synagogue" concept into practice. A Philadelphia group known as the Unstructured Synagogue has been experimenting with this kind of worship for more than a year. The members, who are mostly dropouts from Conservative or Reform synagogues, meet not only for discussions, Hebrew lessons, and the celebration of Jewish holidays but for meals as well. It is thus viewed not strictly as a religious activity but as a new way of expressing Jewish heritage and of giving children a rounded Jewish education. In a typical comment, a member of the Philadelphia group said, "I really feel Jewish, and our group has given me a sense of participating in Judaism in an active way."

Many of the mealtime celebrations involve whole families and include the blessing and lighting of the Sabbath candles. After dinner, there are Israeli folk dances in the living room. Members of this group maintain that they cannot get spiritual fulfillment from the traditional synagogue. "Things that are said and done there," one member commented, "just don't give you a feeling that you've learned something or found another exciting aspect of yourself."

Another idea that seems to be growing and may perhaps constitute a genuine challenge to the traditional Jewish community is the *havurah* or "fellowship" movement, which has groups in Boston, New York, Philadelphia, Chicago, Seattle, and Toronto. These small groups are attempting to create religious communities in which members can study Judaism in an atmosphere of fellowship.

Although the idea had been discussed for years, the "fellowship" movement did not really take form in the United States until 1968 when the Boston Havurat Shalom Community Seminary was opened. The next year the New York Havurah was established, and the other groups soon followed.

While the *havurot* offer intensive study programs, they have rejected the institutional nature of the traditional Jewish seminaries and Hebrew colleges. In the New York Havurah, for instance, students decide what they would like to study. There is no prescribed course of study and practically no minimum number of courses. The direction of each course and the choice of its teacher is left to the students. Since there is no administration to satisfy, unsuccessful courses die a natural death. Thus many of the courses decided upon in the fall are no longer operating in the spring.

There are some who believe the *havurot* are creating new types of Jewish leadership. The Boston Havurat, for instance, which is chartered as an educational, non-profit corporation by the Commonwealth, offers a four-year curriculum leading to the title of *haver* or fellow, and there has been some discussion about the future ordination of rabbis. According to its founder, Rabbi Arthur Green, those students wishing to become rabbis would be given a list of Hebrew texts and secondary sources which they would be required to master. Then they would be examined by a board of rabbis, including those on the faculty and possibly some outside rabbis as well.

Although study is at the center of the *havurah* program, the fellowship movement, in the words of one rabbi, "values the religious quest above the dispassionate search for knowledge." Members of the *havurot* are expected to participate in the religious and communal activities of their groups. Members are supposed to share chores and in general try to work together to create a total religious community. There is much concern about developing meaningful prayer styles. Sabbath services are held every week, and one night a week is set aside for a communal meal. In addition, the New York Havurah has monthly retreats during which the entire group spends a weekend in the country.

The atmosphere at the Boston Havurat has been compared to that of a Quaker meeting. During some services people sit on cushions in the main room of the building and read silently until someone decides to speak out. Members believe this feeling of fellowship strengthens their religious perceptions.

The "fellowship" movement is a search for religious creativity and sense of community, and as such it is a challenge to the old *shul,* or synagogue. As Rabbi Stephen Lerner noted in the Jewish journal, *Conservative Judaism:*

Its existence and its real achievement provide a challenge to the Jewish community. It emphasizes that there is a small but growing number of young people who want to study seriously and to worship intensely. . . . As adolescents they found no place for their commitment in the synagogues, where prayer is rote-reading, community is expressed in suburban soirées, and learning is best described as a Harry Golden lecture. Large synagogues ghettoized the youngsters in the youth service, *de facto havurot*. Rarely did the adult service attempt to integrate youthful energy and creativity into channels of worship or education. Rarely did the youngsters feel that they really shared in synagogue activity. Thus was lost the ideal of the synagogue as a center which could bridge the generation gap and bring together Jews of all ages, as it had for centuries.

He warns rabbis "to surmount their own inertia, the resistance of synagogue boards and ritual committees, and get youth involved in every aspect of synagogue life," adding that they "must make sure that services provide at least some modicum of informality, youthful participation, and creative study."

In Rabbi Lerner's opinion, the *havurot* also constitute a challenge to the seminaries. In the same article, he noted:

More and more students want to study in a setting in which relevance is at least as important as depth, where informality and openness are valued alongside scholarly attainments. . . . If the establishment fails to respond to the request for new styles of learning, more and more students will find supplemental sources of enlightenment or bypass the seminaries altogether.

In addition to the *havurot* study groups, a number of "Free Jewish Universities" have appeared on college campuses. These consist of various courses and activities, which are sponsored by a Jewish organization on campus. In general, the courses are offered outside the conventional university curriculum.

At the heart of the "Free University" philosophy is the belief that students should be involved in decision making, determining not only what to study but for how long and through what techniques. At a typical Free Jewish University, one at the University of Iowa, the courses include:

> The Jew and the Black
> Legends of the Jews
> Conversational Hebrew
> Judaism and History—A Dissenting Voice
> Contemporary Jewish Literature
> Jewish Identity in Transition
> The Jew and the Christian
> Yiddish
> The American Jew and His Self-Image

The director of the B'nai B'rith Hillel Foundation at Boston University, Rabbi Joseph Polak, describes a similar venture on his campus:

> Our Free University started taking on a character and spirit of its own when it became clear after about three weeks of operation that people liked what was happening and were intending to stay. It was nice to go up to Hillel's third floor and find a group of students sprawled on the floor in the hallway, waiting to get into a classroom where a class was running overtime. . . . The atmosphere was characterized by freedom, lightness; students were rarely anxious for the class session to end. There was considerable "intellectual socializing"—students stayed on after classes. Many would come up forty-five minutes before their class just to hang around and talk to someone.

This intense search for new ways of expressing Jewish identity began in the early 1970s and is still on the increase. In the book *The New Jews* James A. Sleeper suggests that the attempt by young Jews to overcome alienation goes beyond having meaning for Jews alone. He writes:

> American youth stands at a new frontier: we have been the beneficiaries and the victims of the old American Dream of material comfort and open opportunity; now, a frightening and exciting world of intangible goals and human redefinition beckons, even as we are pressured by a spiritually hollow society to ignore its call. Our alienation and radical activity—and our sigh—is a suggestion that we are only

beginners in that new world, unable any longer to bear the confines of the old.

On the other hand, much of what is going on in Judaism is going on only on the outer fringes of the traditional Jewish community and as such must be regarded as experimental. But even so these new approaches are genuinely challenging in that they reveal many of the problems faced by the synagogue as a religious institution.

CHAPTER SEVEN

The eloquent spokesman of the civil rights movement, Dr. Martin Luther King, Jr. (above) led his people through sit-ins, marches, and jail-ins until he was felled by an assassin's bullet on April 4, 1968. Possessed of a similar intensity of purpose, the Rev. Jesse L. Jackson (below) has often been hailed as King's successor.

The Black Experience

The black experience is different. Black Americans are struggling for identity in religion, and they are doing so from their own perspective. During the past decade black religious leaders have developed a school of religious thought which puts special emphasis on the past suffering and the present problems of blacks. It is an activist or "committed" theology, and its task, according to one black theologian, Dr. James H. Cone, is "to analyze the black man's condition in light of God's revelation in Jesus Christ with the purpose of creating a new understanding of black dignity among black people. . . ."

According to one teacher of black theology, Dr. William Jones, assistant professor of philosophy of religion at Yale University Divinity School, the black theologian has two fundamental goals. His primary aim is to use theology to improve the black condition, in other words, to use theology as an instrument of social change. His second goal is to demonstrate "the Christian and biblical character of his position." Black theologians differ somewhat in their viewpoints; for instance, some equate black theology with the black power movement, while others do not. But all seek to prove that their positions are consistent with that of the Christian gospel.

For example, Dr. James H. Cone, who is an associate professor of theology at Union Theological Seminary in New York City and one of the best-known of the black theologians, holds the view that Christ's gospel is a gospel of liberation. Thus he claims that:

> If Jesus Christ is in fact the Liberator whose resurrection is the guarantee that he is present with us today, then he too must be black, taking upon his person and his work the blackness of our existence. . . . This means therefore that authentic theological speech arises only from the community of the oppressed who realize that their humanity is inseparable from their liberation from earthly bondage.

According to many black leaders, black theology strikes at the heart of what the black man wants in America today. But what does the black American want? Dr. John H. Satterwhite, a black theologian and professor of ecumenics at Wesley Theological Seminary in Washington, D.C., offered this answer to the question:

> The black man wants a share in everything from the top to the bottom, jobs, homes, etc. This is black power. It has no connotation of "taking over." The black man accepts the concept of "integration" if he is directing the course of events, particularly for himself. That means his "own thing" and he knows what that is and he objects to any program that is handed to him, be it church oriented or a theological kind of attitude.

Since 1938 Dr. Satterwhite has been trying to analyze the nature of Christian faith so that people will understand and respond to the needs of black people. But, he says, if one is to believe in black theology, one must first of all believe in the dignity and redemption of black people.

According to Dr. Satterwhite, there is a basic difference between traditional Christian theology and that of today's black religious leaders. As he puts it:

> Theology is just another worldly activity in the lives of many people. Its purpose is to prepare man to live in another world and therefore it ignores what is happening in this world. Black theology is related to the here and now, not to then and there. That is a tremendous difference. And it is oriented toward the matter of suffering and the prob-

lems that are felt by poor people and black people. Thus the black church and the black religious exponents of today are trying to change things with theology. We are using theology as an instrument of social change in order to change the pattern of life. It is not a case of "taking over" at all; it's just a matter of sharing. We say simply give us some kind of balance, with no restrictions anyplace.

Thus, one of the ultimate objectives of black leaders is to convince the churches to relate religion to social problems, especially the problems of blacks. This is much more important than worship, says Dr. Satterwhite. "To the average white person," he says, "the important thing is worship. It is a belief in saving one by one. Black theology looks instead at the problem of oppression. It looks at the ghetto, at the number of blacks who do not have jobs; who are always fired, who never share in the political power, and it says that is the heart of our oppression. That is where we begin our God talk."

So to black theologians, God is the God of the oppressed. In an article for the Christian Century, Dr. James Cone put it this way: "Any talk about God that fails to take seriously the righteousness of God as revealed in the liberation of the weak and downtrodden is not Christian language."

This is why Dr. Cone has said, "Whether whites want to hear it or not, Christ is black, baby, with all of the features which are so detestable to white society." He means spiritually black, not physically black—black in the sense that black theologians consider Christ the God of black freedom.

Some dangers inherent in this theology have been noted. Miles J. Jones, dean of Virginia Union University's school of theology in Richmond, Virginia, cautioned in *The Christian Century* that "changing our concept of Christ's color is no acceptable substitute for interpreting our experience as black people in the light of what God did and is doing through Christ. Moreover, such 'coloring' is dangerously idolatrous. We need not color God or the Christ black in order to appreciate blackness as an instrument of the divine."

On the other hand, in another article for the same magazine, Dr. William Jones of Yale University Divinity School, explained that black theologians have replaced traditional Christian concepts with novel categories such as the idea of the "black messiah" in order to advance the cause of black liberation and black dignity.

In a similar vein, some black leaders including James Cone, Albert Cleage, and others identify black theology with the economic and politically oriented black power movement. Dr. Vincent Harding, Director of the Institute of the Black World in Atlanta, Georgia, and a leading spokesman for the religion of black power, explained his commitment to black power in the book, *The Religious Situation:*

> Many of the burgeoning black-oriented groups are manned primarily by young men who have been cast out of the restless bowels of a technological society. Now in their teens and early twenties, with little prospect of any meaningful work in the larger society as it now stands, these black youths have begun to find themselves as members of groups dedicated to the protection and development of the ghetto that has so long been their prison. The new vision that Black Power has brought to them may be one of the most important of all its consequences. These were the rejected stones of integration. They had neither the skills nor the graces demanded. They may well become the cornerstones of a renewed black community. . . . So Black Power holds a healthy possibility for the coming of a true religious community. It suggests the destruction of ugly and ironic caste distinctions within the Afro-American community. It encourages the discovery of roots long buried and rejected. It insists that men be true to themselves. It calls a broken people to see its own black section of the mainland. It reveals the gifts of those who were once the scorned members of the black body.

These words were written in 1968, but many blacks consider them to be just as relevant in 1972. Others such as J. Deotis Roberts, Sr., Professor of Theology at the Howard University School of Religion in Washington, D.C., believe attempts to Christianize the black power movement are doomed to failure.

In a sense black theology has always been a part of the black church, but only in recent years has it assumed a definite form. As a mass movement it can be found not only in house churches such as the Black Muslims but also in many of the black Pentecostal, Baptist, and other Protestant churches.

The vast majority of black Americans still attend black churches, and of the nation's approximately 20 million black people, about 12 million are affiliated with black Baptist churches. The major black Protestant denominations are the National Baptist Convention, U.S.A., Inc.; National Baptist Convention of America; Progressive National Baptist Convention, Inc.; African Methodist Episcopal Churches; African Methodist Episcopal Zion Churches; Christian Methodist Episcopal Churches; and numerous Churches of God in Christ and Apostolic Faith Churches. Only about 5 percent of black churchgoers attend "integrated" churches, and there is no organized effort on the part of black leaders to convince black people to join predominantly white churches. Since 1968, however, black caucuses have been engaged in discussions about the roles of clergymen and church officials with reference to the black community.

Thus for the first time black theologians are being listened to by the modern theological movement. But it has been a long time developing, dating from the days when most people thought of black worship in terms of Negro spirituals.

Today music remains one of the main features of black worship. As one observer pointed out:

> In black worship there are no spectators; all are participants, each washed by a wave-like intensity, a succession of rolling peaks that sweep in to pound, pound, the beachhead of your mind. The uncontrolled, integrated use of music, the lyrical, lazy, lean power of the sermon, the heartbeat ecstasy of the invitation—all caress the fibers of your being. And you aren't surprised when a Sister cries out, overwhelmed by the nearness of Jesus, or when a Brother openly, unreservedly pours hot, salty tears into his handkerchief at the confessions of a penitent, come forward by "restoration."

The spirit of the music fills the congregation with a feeling of warmth and community. The atmosphere is charged with emotion, sometimes to the point of overwhelming the worshiper. It has been said that you do not attend a black religious service, but that it attends you. This spirituality is considered by many to be the strength of black worship. It is the real power of the service. As one black preacher explained, "The black church doesn't have the professionalism, the expertise to exist on an organizational basis—emotions hold black worship together."

And much of the emotion comes from the music. Negro spirituals are anonymous. Most are the product not of individuals but of groups, of the pathos and feeling of a people that has known suffering and even despair.

Spirituals are also simple. The words are about life and death, about a brighter tomorrow and a better today. Who can forget the mournful sound of such spirituals as "Go Down Moses," "Swing Low, Sweet Chariot," (about the underground railway), and "Deep River, My Home is Over Jordan" (which referred to freedom via the Ohio River). There is a simple beauty to lines such as these:

> *I've got shoes, you've got shoes.*
> *All of God's chilluns got shoes.*
> *When we get to heaven, gonna put on my shoes.*
> *And walk all over God's heaven.*

Or to these lines from the song "My Lord, What a Morning":

> *. . . when de stars begin to fall*
> *You'll see de worl' on fire*
> *You'll see de moon a bleedin' . . .*
> *Den you'll see de elements a meltin' . . .*
> *You see de forked lightnin'*
> *Den you hear de rollin' thunder*
> *Earth shall reel an' totter*
> *Hell shall be uncapped*
> *De dragon be loosed*
> *Don't you hear the sinners crying?*

Gospel music has been popularized and secularized by such artists as Mahalia Jackson, Ethel Waters, Ray Charles, Dionne Warwick, and Otis Redding, and it has influenced countless numbers of musicians, black and white alike.

Music has always been an integral part of black worship. (Above) A singer entertains the congregation after church. (Below) A woman practices for the church choir.

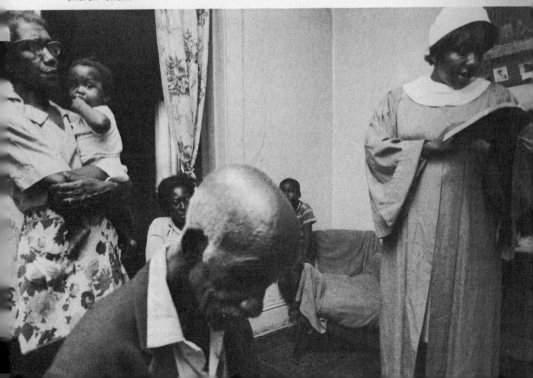

Despite the distinctive aspects of black worship, it has sometimes been said that the black American's religion was handed down to him by the white man. But according to one black minister, the Rev. Thomas Kilgore, Jr., a former president of the predominantly white American Baptist Convention, those who say this just do not know Christian history. As he puts it:

> The church is founded and exists in the experience of Jesus Christ. The heart of this experience was his sacrifice, death, and resurrection. The one person who helped to carry the cross was Simon, the Cyrene, a black man. Saint Augustine, Bishop of Hippo in proconsular Africa (A.D. 396-430), was a black bishop and, beyond that, one of the greatest of the Christian church fathers and philosophers.

On the other hand, the black church in America *was* born out of slavery. As James Cone puts it in *Black Theology and Black Power*:

> The black church was the creation of a black people whose daily existence was an encounter with the overwhelming and brutalizing reality of white power. For the slaves it was the sole source of personal identity and the sense of community. Though slaves had no social, economic, or political ties as a people, they had one humiliating factor in common—serfdom! The whole of their being was engulfed in a system intent on their annihilation as persons. Their responses to this overwhelming fact of their existence ranged from suicide to outright rebellion. But few slaves committed suicide. Most refused to accept the white master's definition of black humanity and rebelled with every ounce of humanity in them.

The coupling of black liberation with divine righteousness has been a continuous theme of black leaders in America. In the 1920s, for example, the theme was voiced by Marcus Garvey, leader of the Back to Africa Movement. If I die, he said, "look for me in the whirlwind of the storm, look for me all around you, for, with God's grace, I shall come and bring with me countless millions of black slaves who have died in America and the West Indies and the millions in Africa to aid you in the fight for Liberty, Freedom and Life."

The Rev. Martin Luther King Jr. was another who contributed immensely to the cause of black freedom and dignity. As one black minister commented, "Long before Negroes could sit in the front of a bus, Martin Luther King sat there mentally." Dr. King was the most eloquent spokesman of the civil rights struggle. He was its prophet, and his message was unselfish love and non-violent resistance. Throughout the fifties and most of the sixties he pressed his civil disobedience campaign, leading his people through sit-ins, march-ins, and jail-ins. He unselfishly gave up his time—and his life for the cause of black humanity.

Theologian James Cone has this to say about him:

> King saw clearly the meaning of the gospel with its social implications and sought to instill its true spirit in the hearts and minds of black and white in this land. He was a man endowed with the charisma of God; he was a prophet in our own time. And like no other black or white American he could set black people's hearts on fire with the gospel of freedom in Christ which would make them willing to give all for the cause of black humanity. Like the prophets of old, he had a dream, a dream grounded not in the hopes of white America but in God. . . . It may appear that white America made his dream into a nightmare by setting the climate for his assassination and later memorializing his name with meaningless pieties. But his dream was grounded in God, man. It was this realization that caused him to say the night before his death: "I've been on the mountain top." Like Moses he did not see the promised land but retained the unshakable certainty that God's righteousness will triumph.

According to Dr. Cone, the black power movement is the result of Dr. King's work, even though King never endorsed the concept. "Black power advocates," says Cone, "are men who were inspired by his zeal for freedom, and Black Power is their attempt to make his dream a reality."

After Dr. King's death, many black leaders hailed the Rev. Jesse L. Jackson, a thirty-year-old Baptist pastor who preaches on Chicago's South Side, as his successor. And indeed Jesse Louis Jackson often sounds a little like King. "We have been the nation's laborers, her waiters," Jackson has said. "Our women have raised her Presidents on their knees. We have made cotton king. We have built the highways. We have died in wartime fighting people we were not even mad at. America worked us for 350 years without paying us. Now we deserve a job or an income."

One of the most persuasive black leaders in America, Jackson commands thousands of loyal followers. His message is economic as well as spiritual. His goal is to build an independent, self-sufficient black community in Chicago. He has found thousands of jobs for blacks and has helped channel millions of dollars into black banks to strengthen the economic base of Chicago's black community. In addition, Jackson has tried to form a coalition with whites, stating that "when we change the race problem into a class fight between the haves and the have-nots, then we are going to have a new ball game."

To emphasize his church's economic message, Mr. Jackson preaches on Saturday instead of Sunday. His service includes a twelve-piece band "to get the people thinking." While he is preaching, he frequently asks for a response: "We black people ought to reappraise our relationship with our black brothers elsewhere. Can I get a witness?" The entire congregation sounds back: "Yes brother. Tell it like it is."

Jackson likes to refer to himself as a "country preacher" and indeed his style is anything but pretentious. A huge man, weighing about 220 pounds and six-foot two inches tall, he wears his hair in the Afro style and prefers bell-bottom trousers, leather vests, and puffy-sleeved, open-neck shirts.

Despite the attempts to equate him with the late civil rights leader, it is clear that Jesse Jackson is not trying to become another Martin Luther King. He has a style of his own. A taut and serious man, he does not appear to possess the warmth of Dr. King and seems to find it unnecessary to smile in public.

Yet despite his somewhat grim appearance his outlook is bright. "Every black man, woman and child must recognize and assert his worth and confidence, his pride and his humility," he has said. "I am what I am and I am proud. Once this 'personhood' is established, 'peoplehood' comes next and 'peoplehood' is made up of persons of integrity who accept a collective identity, a common faith and destiny—people who develop a common political philosophy and begin to buy and sell with in-group priority."

Blacks must keep pushing, he asserts, and says he constantly remembers Dr. King's favorite prayer: "Lord, we ain't what we ought to be, and we ain't what we want to be, we ain't what we gonna be, but thank God, we ain't what we was."

While many black religious leaders are working to solve black problems within the mainstream of American life, others have advocated a complete break with the present society.

Malcolm X, until he converted to "orthodox" Islam, was the outspoken supporter of Elijah Muhammad, the leader of the estimated 100,000-member Nation of Islam. This sect, which has been described by one black theologian as "more of a Christian heresy than a genuine Islamic sect," advocates the separation of blacks from whites and rejects the contention that the two races can be reconciled. In the words of the seventy-five-year-old patriarch, called by his followers the messenger of Allah: "Since we cannot get along with our former slave masters in peace and equality after giving them 400 years of our sweat and blood and receiving in return some of the worst treatment human beings have ever experienced, we believe our contributions to this land and the suffering forced upon us by white America justifies our demand for complete separation in a state or territory of our own."

From his command post on Chicago's South side, the aging prophet watches over some forty Black Muslim mosques and temples throughout the United States and voices his philosophy in an official weekly newspaper called *Muhammad Speaks*. The formal name of the Black Muslims is the "Lost-Found Nation of Islam in the Wilderness of North America," which pretty much says, in just so many words, precisely what this sect's philosophy is.

Articulating this philosophy, and the philosophy of many blacks outside of the Islam movement, Elijah Muhammad told a writer for *Ebony* magazine:

> The thing that is happening now is that Allah is putting the spirit of self in the black man of America. . . . From coast to coast the black man of America now wants to be black. He

> wants to be called black. This is the spirit of God rising in
> our people. It means that they are united and becoming very
> understandable of self. . . . This is what is ultimately bound
> to happen to the American black man. He's bound to become
> united and he is going to be a great nation.

The Muslims believe in practicing what they preach and are
striving to attain economic independence. They own thousands
of acres of land, mainly in Georgia, Alabama, and Michigan.
The sect also operates a dairy, breeds chickens, and has storage
silos, apple orchards, and a cannery. Hundreds of cattle and
sheep graze on Muslim-owned land.

The building in Chicago, where the *Muhammad Speaks*
newspaper is published, takes up some 60,000 square feet of
floor space and has both modern offices and printing equip-
ment. The photo composing room is computerized and a four-
color offset press is used to produce the weekly.

Muhammad himself is a small, thin man, known to violate
some of the rules of grammar when he talks. He lives and
works in a nineteen-room mansion on the South Side of Chicago. Born Elijah Poole in 1897, he was one of twelve children
of a Georgia sharecropper. He renounced his "slave name" as
a youth, and in 1930 in Detroit he met and became the chief
disciple of a mysterious man who at various times called
himself Wali Farrad, W. D. Fard and Farrad Mohammad. Elijah Muhammad has been quoted as saying, "He didn't have to
tell me that He was Allah. When I first met Him, I knew
Him. I recognized Him. And right there I told Him that He
was the one the world had been looking for to come. . . . Then
He put me over the whole thing—the whole nation. He made
me the head of the black man in America."

At first there were informal teach-ins. A hall was rented
and then a temple, a Temple of Islam. The cult grew and one
day, as Muhammad tells it, Fard mysteriously disappeared,
"natural, like a friend leaving another friend." Muhammad became his prophet and, eventually, one of the most powerful
black leaders in America.

Another growing Islamic cult is the "Ahmadiyya Movement," whose faithful are called Ahmadis. The members of

this sect proclaim that they have only adopted a new name, not a new religion. "The Ahmadiyya is a reinterpretation, a restatement of the religion of the Holy Quran and the Holy Prophet Muhammad," says a booklet explaining the religion. The pamphlet also describes the cult's beliefs:

> We are Muslims. We hold beliefs which Muslims must hold and deny the beliefs which Muslims must deny . . . We believe that God is One, without an equal in heaven or on earth . . . Of all divine communications, the most perfect, the most complete, the most comprehensive is the Holy Quran. . . . We believe that death is not the end of everything. Man survives death . . . We believe that divine messengers belong to different spiritual ranks and contribute in different degrees to the fulfillment of the Divine Design. The greatest of all messengers is the Holy Prophet Muhammad. He is the chief of all men, messenger to them all.

The rise of such cults is the result of "racist, socio-economic conditions," Prof. J. Deotis Roberts has written. He also says that the same conditions "have given birth to Black Theology and the religion of Black Power, both of which are dependent upon a reaction to the Christian Faith."

In some instances, he says, blacks have converted to Judaism for similar reasons. At Harlem's Commandment Keepers Congregation of the Living God in New York City, for instance, Afro-American Jews practice Orthodox Judaism and pray in Hebrew, which they consider to be the language spoken by Adam and Eve in the Garden of Eden.

In existence since 1930, this sect contends that the Negroes in America are really Ethiopian Hebrews or Falashas whose name and religion were taken away from them during slavery. The black Jews read the Bible devotedly. They believe that both Jacob and Solomon were black and that they are descended from the union between King Solomon and the Queen of Sheba who started a line of Ethiopian Hebrew kings extending to the "Lion of Judah," Ethiopia's King Haile Selassie, who the black Jews believe is covertly a Hebrew; to the Ethiopians who follow him, however, he is "Defender of the Faith and the greatest leader of Christianity."

The black Jews keep kosher homes, use kosher salt and kosher soap, and refrain from eating non-kosher food, regarding pork, crabs, catfish, and lobsters as unclean. They read the *Torah* in their synagogues, hold weekly services on Friday nights and Saturdays, and celebrate all Jewish holidays. The men wear *yarmulkes*, or skull caps, and *talesim*, or prayer shawls. *Bar-mitzvahs*, or confirmations, are held as in any traditional white Jewish community.

On one point, regardless of the many diverse black religions, all blacks are agreed—that black people no longer have to be apologetic or ashamed of their blackness. On the contrary, blacks believe, as James Cone has written, that "blackness is God's incarnated presence in contemporary America; he will be for black people as he was for oppressed Israelites in Egypt. This is what the gospel means for black people who are search-ing for an interpretation of Christianity that does not deny the worth of blackness."

This "interpretation" is actually a reinterpretation of the contemporary significance of Christianity in the light of black liberation. Only if this is done, black religionists believe, will the black church remain relevant to the American dream of freedom and equality.

PART TWO

The Response

Joyful and unrestrained,
members of a religious
commune practice a folk dance.

CHAPTER EIGHT

After the High is Over

While some observers of the Jesus People doubt that the movement will last, others believe it may infuse new life into established churches. At the 183rd General Assembly of the United Presbyterian Church in the U.S.A., for example, delegates gave a standing ovation to a group of Jesus People led by Dennis Rydberg, pastor of the First Presbyterian Church in San Diego, California. The testimony of the youths had a familiar ring: "I never heard the Gospel in my church. I only heard that Jesus was a great moral teacher, but Christ found me . . . I am a new creature . . . Jesus made my hate disappear. . . . Social change is needed, but before you can get it, you must be changed yourself."

This group, which calls itself the United Presbyterian Liberation Front, urged the delegates to make a new move toward "personal evangelism and leadership training," and their call prompted some observers to sense a new wave of enthusiasm for evangelism at the assembly.

There are other indications that many conventional churchgoers are attracted by the Jesus People's enthusiastic approach to religion. The following are comments by some generally staid church members:

• "I have for some time been distressed at the formal coldness in our beautiful church services—longing for myself and for our youth the joyous feeling the presence of the Holy Spirit brings. It seems that young people have found the way."

123

- "I just hope and pray now that the adults will not quench the Holy Spirit and grieve him to where these youth will not feel comfortable in our churches. I think the time has come for us to accept people and love people, even those we don't understand with whatever experience they have had with God the Father, Son and Holy Spirit."

- "These followers of the Jesus Movement are babes in Christ. It is the duty of mature Christians to help them grow. If, after all, they fail, it will in reality be us, the mature Christians, who have failed."

- "So many of us past thirty have grown cold and complacent . . . we act as though it'd kill us to shout a 'praise the Lord' or shed a tear. We seldom tell anyone that 'Jesus loves them' yet we sit back and worry about the younger generation 'going to the dogs.' Oh, that this movement would reach every nook and cranny of the globe!"

- "These kids are open to the church . . . Now it's just a matter of the churches being open to the kids."

- "The world needs people hung up on Jesus instead of crime, dope, doctrine, or the form of religion."

- "Admittedly, some facets of the phenomenon may be disturbing to those of us who continue to identify with the 'established' segment of the church, but it is now up to churchmen of all traditions to be able to give the new converts the nurture in the faith which they themselves admit they need. If the spiritually newborn cannot receive the necessary encouragement in worship, Bible study, and experience sharing within the existing church, it will be the tragic loss to the latter that they will continue to remain, in most cases, outside the main body of Christianity as a counterculture movement."

This is typical reaction to the Jesus People. But it is not typical of *all* reaction. To the millions of people who continue to identify with the established churches, there is much that is disturbing about this new upsurge of religion, primarily the emotionalism, the disavowal of old values, and the rejection of human wisdom in favor of an almost blind faith that the answers to everything can be found in the Bible.

Furthermore, many church people and other observers of

the Jesus People are questioning the permanence of the movement: How much of this sudden interest in Jesus is a fad? Will
the weaknesses of the Jesus People spell the eventual end of
their movement? Is this, as one Unitarian minister put it, "perhaps the last gasp before the death of religion?" How many of
the new religions will be around five years from now? Will
the new Christians grow into "mature" Christians? Will they
turn to the institutional churches? Is this movement, for that
matter, really religious? Or is it, as has been suggested, some
other kind of impulse under a religious guise?

There is also concern in the Protestant church about how
the average Christian feels today. What does he think of this
latest upsurge of religious movements? How does he feel about
the organized church in its present state? One view was set
forth by Dan Wray Corchran, Associate Professor of Philosophy at Southwest Baptist College in Bolivar, Missouri, in an
article for *Home Missions* magazine:

> Having changed fads more often than the calendar, the aver-
> age Christian feels washed out. The shock approach creates
> anger rather than awakened concern. Even the smallest mat-
> ter becomes a touchy source of irritation. Under such condi-
> tions few people give evidence of prolonged commitment to
> anything. Apathy characterizes not only the church but also
> PTA, civic clubs and social involvements. Why are individ-
> uals so slow to respond in Christian love to human needs?
> One reason might be that they are emotionally drained from
> an overdose of religious fads.
> Fads have polarized the Christian community. The layman
> has lost respect for "faddish" scholarship. If the rational
> content of Christian belief is suspect, then the layman will
> . . . most likely . . . revert to some form of mysticism. The
> choice is unfortunate because irrationalism is more danger-
> ous to faith than is reason. In genuine Christianity reason
> and emotion are partners. What is needed is a combination
> of hard heads and soft hearts, not vice versa. . . . These fads
> have stereotyped religion. Genuine expressions of Christian-
> ity have been blurred, and subsequently our spiritual sensi-
> tivity has been dulled. Faith cannot live where beliefs are
> oversimplified.

The Jesus People, as we have shown, are the most conspicuous of all the new religious adherents, and as far as their move-ment is concerned it is this cry of "faddism" that so often is leveled against them.

For instance, Episcopal minister Malcolm Boyd, who has led attempts to reconcile religion with the needs of society, has charged that cheap publicity gave rise to the movement. "I don't understand people being taken in by it," he has said. "There's always been a Jesus movement. It is nice to create Jesus in one's own image but it is moving into faddism." Ex-tending his criticism to the rock opera *Jesus Christ Superstar,* he asserted, "The next thing Jesus will be a woman. I wonder if she'll be played by Barbara Streisand or Bella Abzug or Nancy Reagan."

In his new booklet *Look Again at the Jesus People,* Dr. Bob Jones III, president of Bob Jones University, calls the move-ment unbiblical:

> If the Jesus of the Jesus Movement is indeed the God of Glory, redeemed people everywhere should be glad of it. If he is another Jesus, Christians should boldly proclaim him to be a fraud and should brand his followers as idolators.

There are few issues, he said, "about which I could write that will bring the same emotional outburst of protest as will a revelation of the unbiblical nature of the Jesus Movement." But he added, that in the mind of a society "conditioned to be-lieve that the Bible is not authoritative and infallible, not abso-lute and unchanging, sincerity covers a multitude of sins." The Jesus movement is "undeniably wicked," he said, "wicked be-cause it speaks not according to the word of God."

Sometimes criticism is mixed with praise. For example, the Rev. Donald F. Hetzler of Chicago, the director of the Na-tional Lutheran Campus Ministry, believes that the movement is helping to create a better climate for campus ministries, but he warns that it may lead to neglect of really crucial issues. In an address before the Lutheran Council in the USA at its sixth annual meeting in Minneapolis in 1972 he stated: "Some of the facets of the Jesus People Movement produce confusion, neglect serious and complicated issues of Christian life in a university setting and are anti-church in their character. Unfortunately, the purported statistical success of such movements is exciting to many who, in a time of general confusion and upset, wish that the Lutheran campus ministry would imitate the methods of these groups."

In some cases, young Jesus advocates arouse real antagonism among older people. The Children of God have provoked the most controversy. These revivalists claim to be an all-volunteer army for Christ, but their detractors, among them many of the Children's parents, say they are "possessed of the devil." Many parents have formed a group called FREECOG (Parents Committee to Free Our Sons and Daughters from the Children of God). This group in turn has been counteracted by "Thank COG" (Thankful Parents and Friends of the Children of God). This group's purpose is to reassure parents "that all of these accusations against the Children just aren't true."

But still the controversy continues to rage. Some parents have tried to retrieve their youngsters or have them committed in an effort to get them out of the COG colonies, which number about 100 in the United States and abroad. Many parents fear that their children are being brainwashed, a charge which some of the Children admit is true. As one put it: "I needed to have my brain washed, and my heart washed too, by the love of Jesus. I knew I was being indoctrinated. That was the whole point: to get indoctrinated to the world of God."

While there has been considerable individual response to the Jesus People, there has been no organized action on the part of the Protestant churches. Many churchmen feel that some response is necessary. Dr. Albert van den Heuvel, Director of Communications of the World Council of Churches, for example, believes that the Jesus People are not so much a threat to the established churches as an accusation. He says that what is needed by way of a proper response is a true friendship or dialogue in the form of recognition, acceptance, and critique.

Dr. van den Heuvel advises the churches to extend more help to the Jesus People, giving them perhaps minimal housing, a place to work, or professional help, either from social scientists or from theologians. Writing in the magazine *Presbyterian Survey,* he observes:

> As always in the Christian Church, the local level is the most important. Only where Christians actually live can the forms of Christian discipline be discovered. Only there does mission find its true form, celebration become commitment and faith disciplined action. The phenomenon of the Jesus People is therefore first of all a challenge to local churches. Here contacts have to be made so that established forms and new experiences can enrich and correct each other. The Jesus People contact each other on the level of "charismata" (gifts of the Spirit), that is they learn from each other how their service can be done better and their experience made known. Would it not be possible for a number of local churches to try "experiments of dialogue"?

Among the issues raised by the Jesus People is the question of church involvement in social action. This is highly controversial, and those who would criticize churches for not responding to important social issues and other modern-day challenges must understand why it has not been at the forefront of social crusades.

One reason is the so-called "suburban captivity of the churches." In an article for *Christian Century* magazine, Dr. Joseph C. Hough, Jr., dean of graduate studies at the School of Theology at Claremont, California, explained the influential thesis set forth by Gibson Winter in the book *Suburban Captivity of the Churches:*

> The churches followed the people into the suburbs, and finding there a mobile and homogeneous constituency, they became centers of quick, folksy familiarity—what Winter calls "active affability" and what I have called "pop Koinonia." Thus harmony became the functional norm of congregational life. For it is easy to see that if serious conflict is generated in the midst of a highly mobile and transient membership, the survival of the institution is called into question. Hence the great hesitancy on the part of local congregations to become involved in anything as controversial as social action.

Perhaps the most important reason why churches are not

leading social crusades, however, is because many church leaders believe the role of the church to be one of comfort rather
than challenge. They feel the church should fill genuine religious needs dictated by the constituency of Protestantism.

Those who would keep the status quo often accuse the
church of "meddling" in civil affairs. "I go to church," said J.
Howard Pew, a member of the board of trustees of the general
assembly of the United Presbyterian Church in the U.S.A.,
"to hear heralded the mind of Christ, not the mind of man. I
want to hear expounded the timeless truth contained in the
Scripture, the kind of preaching that gets its power from
'Thus saith the Lord'." He further added, in a *Reader's Digest*
article:

> To commit the church as a corporate body to controversial
> positions on which its members differ sharply is to divide the
> church into warring camps, stirring dissensions into one
> place where spiritual unity should prevail. . . . If the church's
> "social activists" are to be halted from plunging the church
> . . . into areas where it has no jurisdiction, its concerned lay-
> men and clergymen have to make their voices heard more
> clearly in the high councils of their denominations.

Many would agree. Many disagree. There is a so-called
New Breed in the church which has been pressing for greater,
not lesser, social commitment. They criticize those who would
preserve the status quo, claiming that this prevents the church
from carrying out its true mission in the world, what the New
Breed would probably call "servanthood."

In the midst of this controversy is the claim that there is a
widening gap between the concerns of the clergy and those of
the layman. This claim has made many people wonder whether
the church will survive into the twenty-first century. In his
book, *The Gathering Storm in the Churches,* Dr. Jeffrey K.
Hadden discusses the serious problems posed by man's increasingly pragmatic and secular view of the world:

> The Christian churches today are in the midst of a struggle
> which has every evidence of being the most serious ferment
> in Christendom since the Protestant Reformation. Some have

129

even spoken of the developments of the past few years as the "New Reformation." The general mood of liberal church leaders has been one of euphoria over the prospects of re-uniting Christians who have for centuries been divided over disagreements regarding doctrinal issues. But those who have been unfalteringly optimistic about the prospects of Christian unity have turned their backs on other developments which have been taking place simultaneously—developments which are threatening seriously to disrupt or alter existing church structures.

The optimists have assumed that the ecumenical spirit is a reflection of emerging doctrinal unity. . . . But more important, they have largely ignored at least two alternative explanations of ecumenicism. First of all, is it possible that theological differences have not so much disappeared as they have become irrelevant? If traditional theological doctrines of the Christian churches have become irrelevant, one must ask what it is that has become relevant. And whatever the new relevancy may be, one must further ask if the rank and file of those who call themselves Christians share this new relevance. If the church is in the process of becoming a "new thing" one must ask what this new thing is, as well as the basis of its authority. It is clear that the historical church gathered its authority from many sources, but its strength cannot be divorced from the fact that central to its authority was an elaborate system of rewards and sanctions. The church held the keys to heaven and hell and could say, "No man cometh unto the Father but by me." If the rational-scientific world has not shattered this concept of traditional authority, it has certainly shaken the foundations. . . . Contemporary man is increasingly a pragmatic being, and his acceptance of a particular world view cannot be divorced from pragmatic motivations.

Hadden's concern about the future of the church is shared by many clergymen. Churchmen are becoming increasingly concerned about their roles in the jet-age world. Many are confused by the lack of confidence they receive and are puzzled by questions about the future and about the way churches are almost being forced to change.

At the 1972 meeting of the United States Conference of the World Council of Churches the Rev. Eugene L. Smith, executive secretary of the World Council's New York office told the delegates that "the fundamental issue is who we are . . . the terrifying thing is what many of us do not know." Thus, many clergymen are becoming aware of their own isolation.

Some of the statements of the delegates, on such subjects as violence, salvation, and communication, or "dialogue," with nonbelievers, reflected the difficulties churches are experiencing in responding to modern-day challenges. For example, an Australian Congregationalist, the Rev. David M. Gill, who conducted a two-year study on the Christian responsibility to violence and non-violence, told the delegates that "the Church is extremely confused in the way it analyzes the violence problem, and monumentally inconsistent in offering ethical judgments about it . . . most of our fellow Christians are not consciously acting on such problems at all."

Another church leader, the Rev. Philip A. Potter of Dominica in the West Indies, told those assembled that "the end of Christendom has come. The churches are truly aware of their minority situation. There has been a radicalization of our concerns, and where once we pointed to our mission successes, we now see our weaknesses. . . ."

There seems no doubt that in one way or another churches need to regain self-confidence. This point of view was voiced recently at another conference, a Consultation on Church Union, held in Denver, Colorado. Peter L. Berger, an eminent Lutheran sociologist who spoke out against the smugness of Protestant churches back in the 1950s, told the conferees: "If there is any stance that has marked the Christian community in recent years, it is that of listening." We have listened to the black culture and the youth culture and the Third World cultures, he said, but it is demoralizing to do too much listening "to an entity known as 'modern man' in the expectation that thence will come the redemptive word."

The question that should be asked instead, he said, is this: "What does the church have to say to modern man?" In this regard, he maintained, what is needed is a stance of authority by those "who have come to terms with their own experience and who are convinced that in however imperfect a measure, they have grasped some important truths about our human condition." If a true renaissance of religion comes, he added, the leaders will not be "the people who have been falling all over each other to be relevant to modern man. Ages of faith are marked not by dialogue, but by proclamation."

Despite the problems the church is experiencing, many clergymen believe much of the talk about the church's dying is simply rhetoric. After spending two years working on Project Understanding, an experimental educational project in Southern California, Dr. Joseph Hough concluded that many congregations are "experiencing the liveliest time of their existence." He believes this is "due to churchmen's increasing willingness (or at least their recognition of the need) to face conflict and controversy as part of congregational life." Thus in Dr. Hough's opinion, "it is certainly true that most congregations are encountering difficulties, but (it is doubtful) that even a well-organized plan of attack could kill the churches. They are here to stay, much alive and, in some cases, undergoing significant changes."

At the same time, however, Dr. Hough's study noted the widespread acceptance of the "comfort" view of the church:

> In almost every church, we met resistance to our anti-racist programs on the grounds that people seek relief from the pressures and conflicts of life in the services of the church. Anything that emphasized problems or highlighted issues was considered counter to the group's religious needs. . . . Genuine, felt religious needs often form the basis for resistance to the introduction of conflict-producing change into the life of the church. People do suffer, die, have anxieties, and they need comfort. Religion is still seen as a "rock in a weary land," a comfort to the weak and heavy-laden, and a presence to the lonely. Interestingly enough, we discovered that a number of laymen who are active in secular social change organizations shared this fundamentally quietistic and comfort-oriented view of the role of the church today.

There is no doubt that the questioning of the church's role does lead to tension, both within and without the church. It can keep many of the socially conscious from attending church. But according to Dr. Hough, there does not always have to be a choice between "comfort" and "challenge." He believes that "a plural understanding of religious needs and a legitimation of pluralistic expressions of religious vitality could enable the local church effectively to do both."

Yet despite the criticism that the churches are not responding to all the challenges facing them, there is no doubt that they are more socially conscious than ever before. Church leaders are speaking out about issues of national and international importance, including questions of race, labor, and war. The war in Vietnam, for instance, has long been regarded as a religious and moral issue. There is also a growing indication that more and more churches are sponsoring projects to help under-developed communities in the United States and abroad.

Among numerous humanitarian programs is one sponsored by the United Presbyterian Church in the U.S.A. Its goal is to raise $70 million in the decade of the 1970s for a Fund for the Self-Development of People. Similar programs are being sponsored by the Episcopal Church, the United Methodist Church, the Christian Church (Disciples of Christ), and many other denominations.

The need to expand the social role of the churches was voiced at the 1966 World Council of Churches' Conference on Church and Society, and the number of projects has been growing ever since. In 1968, for instance, the World Council joined forces with the Vatican through the agency of a joint Commission on Society, Development and Peace (SODE-PAX) and more recently, in the United States, the National Council of Churches established a Task Force on Action-Education for Justice, Liberation, and Development.

Another organization, which is aimed primarily at helping minority groups in the United States, is the Interreligious Foundation for Community Organization (IFCO). Founded in 1966 and supported by about fifteen church bodies, this group expects to raise about $1.5 million in 1972 from churches, foundations, and individuals.

To those who contend that the churches are incapable of moral leadership, there is a sign of hope in the recent action taken by the 185,000-member Church of the Brethren, which decided to sell all of its stock holdings in firms with military contracts. Holding all war to be sinful, the Church announced that it would divest itself of some $800,000 worth of securities in nine firms.

This action "should strengthen the resolve of those within the churches who work for peace, justice and human libera-tion," commented Frank White, executive head of the Corpo-rate Information Center of the National Council of Churches, which recently published a study showing that eleven religious bodies held $200 million worth of securities belonging to twenty-nine of the sixty leading military contractors with the Defense Department.

Then too, as an example of relief and service projects, there is the Seventh-Day Adventist Welfare Services (SAWS) which dispensed $14.7 million in relief materials during 1971. This disaster-aid organization served thirty-six countries in ad-dition to the United States and Canada. The largest amount, a total of more than $11.8 million, went to Peru. SAWS has 672 centers in the United States and Canada, and its members gave more than 4.1 million hours to humanitarian work and served more than 2.27 million people in North America alone.

In other social action projects, the American Baptist Service Corporation is working in hundreds of different areas and is spending millions of dollars to provide planning, fund gather-ing, and co-ordination for the nonprofit housing programs of other denominations. Another large body, the United Church of Christ, has made deposits in black-owned banks in New York City and has bought shares in a corporation which finances housing and other key development programs in the United States, Canada, and Latin America.

Many churches have raised funds to provide housing for the elderly, to build hospitals, and to renovate houses for poor people. This is not strictly a church effort. In one project, the Adopt-a-Building effort begun in East Harlem, New York, in 1969, hundreds of volunteers from more than seventy churches, synagogues, corporations, community agencies, and tenant organizations have helped tenants living in deteriorating buildings. This interfaith program also has been successful on New York's Lower East Side, the West Side, Bedford-Stuy-

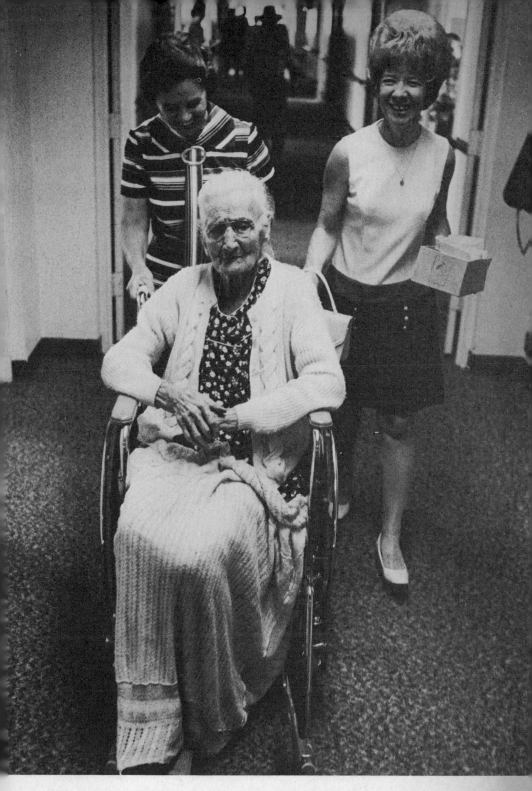

Members of the Mission Action group of the First Baptist Church in Bellevue, Nebraska, spend much of their free time visiting patients in hospitals and nursing homes.

vesant, Ocean Hill-Brownsville, and Bronx sections of the city.

Projects such as these often go unnoticed. Much more national attention has been paid to the efforts of a growing number of churches to produce more imaginative and innovative worship services. For instance, encounter groups and sensitivity groups are now in vogue in some churches on Sunday mornings. And in other churches there are folk masses and plenty of singing, guitar playing, and hand clapping. "In our church," said one young Methodist, "we had the laying on of hands. I am really open to this healing thing." Another young worshipper added, "I am for plenty of singing, clapping, dancing, and bright colors."

It may be too early to determine whether innovative forms of worship are putting new life into the church or attracting new members. One large church association encouraged new forms of worship and found that its membership declined by almost 17,000 that year. Other churches have had to struggle with constant dissension arising from attempts to change styles of worship that are deeply rooted in tradition.

There may be admiration for what many of the young are saying or for what they have inspired some churches to do, but great numbers of people continue to be skeptical about anything radically new. Sometimes they are moved to anger, as expressed, for instance, by one "wage-earning, family-raising, mortgage-paying Presbyterian" in a letter to *Presbyterian Life* magazine:

> Nowhere does there seem to be any concern by the "freaks" for the anguish, heart-break, and unhappiness their pre-dawning behavior has brought upon all those whose lives they have touched. . . . In this time it seems the prodigal son wants the calf delivered to the coffee-house—cooked. . . . Who doesn't privately dream of drifting around the country without responsibility, traveling by speedy Honda, or sleeping under the stars in sunny California while at the same time being heralded as a discoverer of Truth? Communal living isn't a new thing, but communal living sponsored by the resources of the community is free-loading.

What *is* the younger generation coming to, and how are the

churches responding? There simply is no single or all-embracing answer. So much depends on where you look. If, for example, it happens to be Collingswood, New Jersey, you will find the Rev. Philip Everett Worth whose team of five ministers is trying to create an atmosphere of Christian fellowship. According to "Gus" Gilbert, chairman of the church's commission on education, "Around here a kid who declares for Christ and Christian service is a hero."

One group of high schoolers who had been trained by the church's youth director opened a coffee house for Collingswood youth called "The Way Out." Local police were so impressed with it that they tried to persuade the church to make it permanent.

Similar action is being taken by many Methodist churches of evangelical persuasion, which generally are not experiencing the decline in attendance and finances that many congregations of traditional denominations have suffered over the last few years. While hard times have been affecting other churches, evangelistic churches and organizations report rising levels of interest: Evangelistic literature is thriving, Bible-centered institutions are prospering, and evangelical membership is up about 3 percent.

The farther west one goes, particularly in southern California, the better is the reception to innovative forms of worship and church service. The pastor of one Baptist church in Beverly Hills preaches to youth in their language: "Christ wants to give you the greatest life going. He wants to fill you with himself, not drugs. God isn't some cosmic bully trying to do you in. He loves you and wants you to groove on him, not on something you put into your body for kicks. Think about it, man. It's your life and your choice."

Much of the response is taking place outside of the organized church, but as Paul Curtis, director of Los Angeles Teen Challenge, a youth outreach ministry related to the Assemblies of God, explained:

> We're interested in winning young people to Jesus Christ and we don't care what they look like, how they smell or where they come from. Until a person is dealt with in his

Innovative services such as this one which combines modern dance and religious movement are one means by which a growing number of Protestant churches are seeking to stimulate greater interest in their activities.

highest dimension, the spiritual, he has not been reached. We try to minister to the physical, psychological and spiritual needs of the teen-agers. On the West Coast there is a swinging, drug-oriented culture. California is two years ahead of the rest of the United States in these pursuits. Every day a kid hooked on drugs wanders into one of our five Teen Challenge centers, looking for help. We don't gang up on him. One person usually talks with him and helps to guide him through our rehabilitation program. We present him with the promises of Jesus Christ and seek to lead him to become a Christian.

In the final analysis, some observers believe that the very people who are attacking the church will come into the organized Christian community. Dr. Martin E. Marty, Professor of Modern Church history and Associate Dean of the Divinity School at the University of Chicago, for example, says that if this happens both the church and the new movements will benefit: "Social activism by churches thins out if it doesn't have a new input of religious experience. If our churches want a new input, they have no choice except to absorb the 'Jesus People.' In the final analysis we must become a synthesis of heart and reason."

There already is some assimilation taking place, primarily among Pentecostal churches and scattered Presbyterian and Baptist congregations as well as Pentecostalist elements in the Episcopal and Catholic churches and other large established Protestant bodies.

But for the Jesus people and others, the real test is yet to come. How will they act after the trip is over, when they begin to come down from their emotional high? It is the hope of many that they will become part of a healing Christian community—The Church.

CHAPTER NINE

Laying his hands upon the head of each man, Pope Paul VI greets sixty-one newly ordained Roman Catholic priests.

Changes in The "Unchangeable" Church

Twenty years ago, the Catholic church was viewed as the "unchangeable" church. Today every tradition is being shaken. The idea of a married priesthood is being discussed as is the notion of elected bishops. Some orders of nuns have raised their hems or doffed their habits. Others have begun to direct their affairs without asking for guidance from priests or bishops. The liturgy is now being read in English, and Catholic laymen are speaking out about social action, parochial schools, and parish organizations in what has been called the "beginning of the beginning" of change within the church.

The church continues to oppose abortion and divorce and to set forth strict rules for behavior, but many of the things Catholics used to confess are no longer sins. It is no longer a sin to eat meat on Friday, for instance, or to miss Mass on Sunday or not to go to confession (unless one has committed a mortal sin). Today a minority, not the majority, of Catholics go to confession, and most go as infrequently as once every two months. Moreover, there is growing evidence that some Catholics think their children still can be saved if they leave the church and that many would not be willing to spend more money to maintain parochial schools if the government did not advance funds to do so.

One Catholic expressed the feelings of many when he said, "It is like a different religion now."

Another asked, "How can you listen to God with all those

guitars? We've got everything in church these days—long hair, noise, liturgy in English, social action—everything but reverence."

On the other hand, there is this comment from a Connecticut Catholic. In a letter to one of the nation's largest newspapers, he wrote:

> I was born and raised a Roman Catholic. I was an altar boy. I never missed mass, I went to confession and communion regularly, I ate fish on Friday, I thought there were two kinds of people: Catholics and non-Catholics . . . I met a Catholic girl and we had a Catholic wedding. Then something happened. Quite a few things, in fact: Pope John and Vatican II and Women's Lib and Black Power and Campus Unrest. And for us: pregnancy. Three of them. I was 29 at the time, my wife 25, and we realized at this rate we could have about twenty children. So the question was: how do we avoid pregnancy? How do we avoid it as Catholics? . . . If you remove one brick from a structure of belief, other bricks begin to fall. After our fifth child we pulled that first brick and started practicing birth control. . . . For about a year I didn't go to church, and I stopped being a Catholic. I guess you have to know first what you don't want before you can begin to know what you do. There were some things I missed during this twelve-month sabbatical, but there were more things I was glad to be rid of. The biggest thing I was rid of was authoritarianism. . . . We . . . still consider ourselves Catholics, but no longer Roman ones. We still believe in God, but he's no longer enshrined in the Vatican or a candlelit church. We still go to Mass, but the liturgy is no longer bound by brick and mortar. We still take communion, but the Eucharist is no longer shaped like a smoothly flattened ping pong ball and can now be a slice of store bread or a broken piece of matzo. We still go to confession, but those we "sin" against we ask forgiveness from directly. We have not stopped listening to the experts altogether, just stopped believing them altogether. I guess our Roman days are over, and our roaming ones just begun.

Not everyone would agree with these statements, but few will question that the church is in a state of theoretical ferment and that the emphasis today is on updating, reform, ecumenical dialogue, and self-knowledge.

The tradition-breaking Second Vatican Council, which was summoned by Pope John XXIII in 1962 and ended in 1965, unleashed great forces for change. It has been said by some that Vatican II and the Synods (meetings) that followed in 1967, 1969, and 1971 gave birth to a "new breed" of Catholic scholar. Numerous specific changes have occurred. Around the world, for instance, the Mass is now delivered in the local language. But the most conspicuous change is that the old image of the obedient Catholic is rapidly fading.

One of the problems of formulating a response to the demands for change is to decide first of all which are the real problems. What is discussed by the press or what draws the most attention may not be the real or the most crucial problem. So much has been written and said about the controversial issues of celibacy (a majority of American priests do favor optional celibacy) and birth control and about unhappy and frustrated priests that it is easy to see how other issues can become clouded.

According to one eminent Catholic sociologist, Father Andrew M. Greeley of the University of Chicago's Center for the Study of American Pluralism, "The fundamental crisis of the American Church at the present time is not structural, it is not sexual, it is not even in the primordial sense of the word religious; it is theoretical."

In Father Greeley's opinion, a crisis has arisen in the American church because old theories have collapsed so quickly that there has been no time for new theories to develop. The American church and the American priesthood is facing a "time of confusion, disorientation, and chaos," he maintains. "We lack theory, direction, goals, values, and models of appropriate behavior. We do not have the leaders, lay, clerical, and hierarchical, who can communicate a sense of direction to us; we do not have scholars who can evolve new theories; we do not have prophets, poets, saints, who can create splendid new visions to attract the minds and hearts of all of us."

His view of the problem is that Catholic theory—that is, the goals, the values, and the basic assumptions of people—has in the past been so rigid and so taken for granted "as to be-come almost totally unconscious."

Up until about 1960, Greeley has noted, Catholic theory emphasized strict discipline, unquestioning obedience, loyalty, certainty, and an incapacity to change. It tended to cast suspi-cion on anything outside of the church and, while stressing a comprehsnive Catholic community, discouraged any re-exami-nation of fundamental principles.

Within this framework, according to Father Greeley, the parish priest knew the way he was supposed to behave. As he puts it:

> The priest taught in school, said Mass, heard confessions, visited the sick, buried the dead, prepared young people for marriage, moderated parish organizations, tried to straighten out 'bad' marriages, tried to reclaim 'fallen away' Catholics, provided some sort of minimal instruction for those who were going to public schools, spent his day off with clerical classmates, made sure that there was somebody always 'on call' in the rectory, and, if it was a particularly progressive parish, greeted the people in the back of the church after Sunday Mass.

But today, he says, the faithful are increasingly questioning the authority of the church. Young priests in particular are prone to question the hierarchy, not being confident in it and so not looking up to it. If an individual bishop does enjoy the confidence of his priests, it is more than likely not because of the bishop's office, Father Greeley claims, but because by his behavior the bishop has earned his priests' respect. In some dioceses, he observes, "the only power the bishop has left is the power of the purse strings, and unless the present erosion of authority is arrested, it is no apocalyptic prediction to say that by 1980, there will be no such thing as ecclesiastical authority in the American Church (except over the checkbook) save in those dioceses where bishops have been able to overcome the skepticism, not to say, cynicism of their priests by their own efforts."

Father Greeley believes that a new foundation in the form of new theory is needed. In his words:

Priests from more than 100 Catholic groups meet to form an Association; these Associations are independent of diocesan bishops and thus constitute a challenge to the traditional church structure.

Three Catholic nuns relax in their new suburban home after moving out of the convent; they work at regular jobs during the day and attend to their church duties at night.

The history of the last five years of the Church ought to be sufficient indication that there are no quick and easy solutions; there is no chance of going back to the old certainties, and there is no shortcut that will enable us to escape the hard, lengthy work of going back to the very beginning and asking once again the most basic and primal questions. The national hierarchy can issue statements from now until judgment day and no one will listen to them unless they begin to see . . . both understanding that the old theories and the old cliches are useless and the beginnings of a new theory which gives direction in the midst of confusion, hope in the midst of uncertainty, and light in the midst of darkness.

Another problem facing American Catholicism is the crisis in parochial schools. Catholic school enrollment has been dropping since 1965, down 5.6 percent between 1970 and 1971; down 8.2 percent between 1971 and 1972. According to the Official Catholic Directory, the number of schools is also declining, from 13,196 in 1965 to 11,021 in 1972. Not long ago they were closing at as high a rate as one a day.

Already more than half of the Catholic school-age children in the United States are receiving their religious training outside of the Catholic school system. Increased tuition fees are part of the reason for student loss. With the question of tax credits, tuition reimbursements, and equitable sharing in new federal programs still up in the air, Catholic parents are being forced to decide whether they feel a Catholic education for their children is necessary. Other reasons given by experts for the problems of parochial schools include the increased quality of public school education, the declining number of teaching nuns, and parental dissatisfaction with the nature of religious training.

The result is that a growing number of Catholic children are growing up without any formal religious training. In one effort to correct the situation, the Archdiocese of Washington conducted a self-study in which it was recommended that increased funds be channeled into Confraternity of Christian Doctrine (CCD) programs of after-school and weekend religious instruction. The report also urged greater emphasis on adult religious education programs.

The CCD programs, however, are largely in the hands of volunteers, and when Catholic schools have closed, enrollment in the CCD programs has not always increased.

It may still be too early to tell precisely what role Catholic schools will play in the decade of the seventies and beyond. Taking an optimistic view, the president of the National Catholic Educational Association, C. Albert Koob sees Catholic education in this era as probably "as healthy an apostolate as ever before in its history." In an article for the Jesuit magazine *America,* he asserted:

> Catholics are learning not to judge health by numbers. We have come to grips with the hard reality that schools cannot be taken for granted. The evidence is pretty strong that many Catholics want schools. This means they must persuade their coreligionists that such schools are justified, find ways to pay for them, live with the new philosophy that makes the school more of a service to society than a self-perpetuating institution, and then be certain that the program of the school is extended to serve adults and other children not in those schools. And this is exactly what is happening on a fairly large scale. . . . Ways are being sought to solve the financial problems that threaten to undo all institutions at this time.

The numerical projections are less promising: Catholic elementary school enrollment is expected to drop to 2.15 million by 1975 and to 1.4 million by 1980. This would be a 60 percent decrease within ten years. Secondary school enrollments appear to be headed for a 30 percent decline over the same period, from over one million in 1970 to 822,000 in 1975 and to less than 700,000 by 1980. On the other hand, Catholic school operating costs per pupil for 1975-76, for example, are expected to zoom to $575 on the average for the elementary level and to $950 for the secondary level.

Public aid for full-time Catholic education seems to hold the most hope for reversing this gloomy projection, but more important perhaps will be the attitudes of Catholic administrators, educators, parents, and members of the public toward educational and financial innovations.

Young people break into song at a Catholic folk mass.

In an April, 1972, issue of *America* Ernest Bartell, the Catholic educator who administered the national economic study of Catholic elementary and secondacy schools for the President's Commission on School Finance, observed that Catholics will back educational initiatives if they are sufficently motivated. He wrote:

> Since they now support the operation of their schools with subsidies that amount to little more than one percent of their family incomes, an increase of only one percent in voluntary contributions could almost double existing operating subsidies to Catholic education.

The educational crisis is, however, just one aspect of the problem. Converts to Catholicism are also down, as is the number of infant baptisms. Furthermore, there is some evidence that a large number of Catholics in their late teens and early twenties do not attend mass regularly.

During the past six years there has been a real modification of Catholic ritual. Thus, since some basic reform of the liturgy has been carried out, it appears ironic that so many of the young should be rebelling. On the other hand, many members of the Catholic clergy do feel that the church has made errors. In the opinion of one priest:

> [The church] has been making serious mistakes in presenting the Eucharist to young people in terms of a mortal sin obligation. In all areas of their lives we expect them to grow and develop, but not in this area of eucharistic life. From the beginning, from age seven, we have been expecting full and unswerving fidelity. There is no process of development allowed; neither is there choice or freedom in this one privileged area.

In a similar vein, a report conducted by the Archdiocese of Washington recommended that the folk mass, which had been regarded with suspicion by many members of the archdiocese be recognized as a "legitimate and desirable" form of worship. The self-study report said, "The practice of priests who would deny youth the options approved by the church for variety on Sundays and other special occasions should be prohibited."

The church hierarchy also has internal problems. Young priests cannot be ordained fast enough; five years ago there were twice as many seminarians as there are today. Thus, priests who die, retire, or resign are not being replaced by an equal number of seminarians. Furthermore, since the late 1960s, approximately forty-five seminaries have closed, and the number of seminarians has dropped about 13 percent.

Father Francis Lonsway, a Franciscan priest and assistant executive officer of the secular American Association for Higher Education, has had this to say about the troubles in "the sems":

> Youths today do not think priests are doing the job that has to be done; they see secular agencies doing more than the church. Youths seek a self-effacing ministry. You see this in their attraction to Middle East religions. Often they don't find self-effacement in the church. Not only do we find fewer students going to the seminary, we find almost 40 percent of the new seminarians drop out. Seminary newcomers come to realize for the first time how terribly human the church is. There *are* favored people; the wealthy, the bishops. It comes as a psychological shock when the seminarians see the difference between what is preached and what is lived.

In an effort to attract more students, some seminaries are changing their rules about life styles. At the Catholic University of America, for instance, student priests are allowed to wear long hair and beards. They can come to classes in tie-dyed shirts and faded blue jeans, sleep as late as they want, and decorate their rooms with psychedelic posters if they feel like it; not so long ago they would have risen shortly after dawn and lived an obedient, semi-cloistered life.

Many bishops have been disturbed by these changes, and some have withdrawn their financial backing of the university's once prosperous Theological College. Consequently, TC is suffering from the same problems that are affecting other seminaries throughout the country.

Still, Father Ed Frazer, the rector of Catholic University's Theological College, defends the changes: "People expect un-

Children are about to receive Holy Communion at an outdoor Mass.

derstanding or empathy from a priest. They expect him to have a feel for the world's real problems. Many priests today lack these things. By not shielding the seminarian, we give him a chance to learn what people's real problems are and to see if he can relate to them."

The search for "unshielded" young men led one recruiter of seminary candidates to *Playboy* magazine, where he placed a full-page $10,000 ad that asserted: "You are already a Trinitarian. You who have love to give and the courage to offer it, you are already a Trinitarian. Come work with your brothers. Come home." Many of Father Joseph Lupo's fellow Trinitarians disapproved of the idea, but faced with a sharp decline in the number of new seminarians, Father Lupo decided to "go where the men are."

Father Lupo, who is vocations director of the Italian order, would not disclose the number of letters received from interested young men, but he said, "Let's put it this way. We're ecstatic. . . . Since the ad came out some people have told me, 'These are the affluent, sophisticated men, the men who read Playboy.' And I say, 'that's OK, that's the kind of young man who's sensitive and knows what is going on in the world, the kind of young man we need.' "

Another crucial departure from Catholic tradition took place in the late 1960s when priests began organizing in groups known as Associations. Since many of these Associations were independent of diocesan bishops, they constituted a challenge to traditional church structure. In an effort to gain greater control over the priests, many bishops began encouraging the establishment of Senates, which were also composed of local priests.

According to Father Laurence Maddock, chairman of the board of the Association of Chicago Priests, the Senates were a "zone defense" thrown up to hold in the independent Associations. In the minds of many, he notes:

> The Senates . . . became the company unions which were fostered to contain the independent Associations. . . . Senates soon outnumbered Associations by a four-to-one margin, or better. They became the nation's most influential councils of

priests. It looked like everything was under control again. . . .
Then a funny thing happened one September day in 1968.
The Senates formed together into an independent, associa-
tion-like, organization called the National Federation of
Priests' Councils.

In the words of Father Maddock, "To the surprise and oc-
casional consternation of their bishops, some 100 Senates had
signed up for membership in the NFPC with 25 to 30 Associations." Today priests from all parts of the country belong to
this Federation.

But the formation of the Federation was only the beginning.
Soon priests in the NFPC began to further displease their bishops by calling for greater freedom. They voiced their displea-
sure with the status quo by making demands such as these:
"We want to vote for bishops in the future . . . We want the
right to be able to get married . . . The power of priests' Senates should be more than merely consultative . . . The hierarchy lacks leadership."

Although the church hierarchy has made no sweeping re-
forms in response to these demands, in one area it has made
some changes. In May, 1972, after four years of intensive
study and consultations, the Vatican issued a new set of rules
to govern the nomination of bishops. The rules do not provide
for the election of bishops, nor do they allow bishops to consult
with groups such as priests' councils as this might give the appearance of an election. But they do involve more people in
the process of nominating candidates. For example, bishops
now have the option of consulting with individual priests and
laymen in their dioceses about the kind of man needed. Any
bishop may send a nomination directly to the Pope, and national bishops' conferences may now comment on and add to
the list of local nominations.

The lists of nominees will still be sent to the country's papal
representative, who retains the job of investigating the candidates and can make nominations of his own. Under the new
rules, however, the papal representative must confer with
other clergymen in that country. In addition, he may consult
with laymen if he so desires. Finally, the new rules retain the

Pope's option of choosing a man whose name is not on the lists. The Vatican's action on the selection of bishops was hailed by some Catholic progressives as a step in the right direction.

Still there is discontent in the ranks of the clergy. Many priests are so displeased with the existing order that they have left the priesthood altogether; during the past eight years some 25,000 priests, curates, and even a few biships have left their calling in various parts of the world.

So many are the problems of the Catholic priesthood today that one theologian has posed the questions: Why priests? Why should a special Church "office" be needed today? Why, in a pluralistic and democratic society, should there be a polarity between office and people?

Hans Kung, professor of Dogmatic and Ecumenical Theology, Director of the Institute of Ecumenical Studies at the University of Tubingen, Germany, and one of the Catholic church's most controversial theologians, says in his recently published book *Why Priests?* that he would rather speak about Church ministry than about Church office, for the word ministry has a humbler sound and carries less of a link with authority and power. "Today it is harder than ever to define the essence of Church office," he writes. "And there is no doubt that the identity crisis of many pastors, curates and even bishops is based not least of all on the fact that one no longer knows what a priest, pastor or bishop really is, why he is a priest, pastor or bishop. Is he primarily a liturgist or preacher or organizer? Is he more a catechist or someone who offers practical assistance? Is his activity oriented more toward the congregation or more outward toward society?

In his book Father Kung makes the following bold challenges:

> The Church's ministry of leadership does not have to be a full-time ministry: It need not be a profession in every case . . . someone who takes on the headship of the congregation as a second vocation (part-time priest) while continuing his occupation as laborer, technician, civil servant, teacher, doctor (after the example of the apostle Paul) represents a pos-

sibility at least as serious as the diaconate revived by Vatican II. As many people's free time increases, a part-time ministry might be very practical, especially for non-territorial congregations. It would no longer be a question of turning priests into workers (worker-priests), but of making workers priests. This would mean new categories of congregational leaders, whose education would not have to consist in an all-round theological training but would certainly have to be aimed at definite objectives and adapted to the intellectual level of the community concerned.

The Church's ministry of leadership does not have to be for life. It need not in every case be a life's work. . . . There seems to be no reason why ministry in the Church— full-time and still more part-time—cannot under certain circumstances quite well be a *temporary ministry*. This need no more be detrimental to the seriousness of the commitment than service for a limited time in the Peace Corps or in aid to underdeveloped countries. . . .

And priests, claims the outspoken theologian, do not have to be celibates to effectively carry out their ministry. For some special tasks which involve traveling and long absences single priests would be especially useful. But, he notes:

Even those in the Catholic Church who still defend celibacy as compatible with the freedom of the gospel of Jesus Christ and also as pastorally expedient will admit that it is a matter of a purely ecclesiastical law from the Middle Ages. . . . This law (of celibacy) contradicts not only the original Church order based on freedom but also the modern understanding of human rights and individual liberty. This tradition, peculiar to the Latin Church . . . tries to ignore the fact that in every age of the Church's history from the first to the twentieth century there have been married Catholic presbyters who exercised their ministry well, often in an exemplary fashion. . . .

If the day of the all-obedient priest is over, so is the time when nuns unquestioningly carried out directives from the male hierarchy. The stereotype of the Catholic nun moving about in long robes, speaking only when spoken to, and looking as though she were part of another world, is gone—or at least fast going.

There are about 150,000 Catholic nuns in America, and in the spirit of Vatican II, they have become a strong new force in the church. Widening their social apostolate, they have called for greater social commitment by the church. Furthermore, many American nuns have begun to feel that cloistered community living and distinctive religious attire are preventing them from reaching the people they want to help. Thus, in some orders there has been a gradual relaxation of strict monastic rules.

Many nuns have donned modern garb and entered new professions without completely leaving the convent. Others have abandoned their orders to form "noncanonical" communities, which are outside the reach of church authority. Today there are at least fifty of these groups in the United States; the membership of these groups ranges from 3 to nearly 300. In most cases sisters belonging to these experimental communities rent apartments or houses, perhaps sharing with one or two members. There are no formal, structured communities. The nuns find jobs to pay their own way and write private commitments to Christ instead of taking formal vows.

The new nuns have also branched out beyond the traditional professions of teaching, nursing, and running orphanages and old-age homes. Many are counseling drug addicts, working in prisons, studying law, and joining organizations like the Job Corps. Others are working for crusaders like Ralph Nader and Cesar Chavez.

The church hierarchy so far has shown no sign of condoning these departures from tradition. In the summer of 1971, Pope Paul VI spoke out against changing the "essential commitments" of religious life. The Vatican has also forbidden nuns to exchange their habits for secular dress.

On the other hand, some local churches in the United States have upgraded the role of nuns. In many dioceses, including Detroit, Toledo, Houston, and Kansas City, Missouri, nuns have been given pastoral assignments that involve counseling and management duties, tasks formerly performed only by priests.

Moreover, some people in the church believe that women

should be on equal footing with men in the clergy. If there can be priests, they wonder, why not priestesses? Already, there is active discussion about appointing women deacons, and many Catholic scholars see no serious objection to women priests. For example, Hans Kung, one of the liberal Catholic theologians, states in *Why Priests?*:

> Full participation of women in the Church's life, on the basis of equal rights, is something that belongs to a suitably renewed Church today. This means not only including women as coresponsible in the different advisory and decision-making bodies . . . but also the admission of women to all the Church's special ministries and to ordination. . . . Sociological reasons have been advanced against the ordination of women for a territorial and perhaps even more for a non-territorial ministry of leadership, but no decisive theological reasons have been presented.

Congregations today, says Dr. Kung, are "limping along" behind the times. Experience in the political realm proves that "inhibitions and objections regarding the full equality of women, explicable in terms of social psychology, can be overcome in the course of time."

According to some scholars, even Jesus was a feminist. Leonard Swidler, editor of the Journal of Ecumenical Studies and professor of Catholic Thought at Temple University, notes:

> The Gospels give no evidence of Jesus ever treating women as inferior to men . . . contrary to the current attitude, Jesus clearly thought that the "intellectual life" was proper for women, that the role of women was not limited to being "in the home." This was made clear during his visit to the home of Martha and Mary. . . . It is clear from the Gospels that Jesus vigorously promoted the dignity and equality of women in the midst of a very male-dominated society: Jesus was a feminist, and a very radical one. Can his followers attempt to be anything less?

Thus it appears that the authority of the Catholic hierarchy is increasingly being challenged. Many priests, nuns and laymen are becoming more independent than they have ever been.

In this atmosphere of uncertainty and change, Pentecostalism is finding limited acceptance in today's Catholic Church. Sociologist William McCready, for example, observed that:

> The increasing division between the religious and the hierarchical dimensions within the Church has opened up opportunities for choosing options that never before existed. . . . Increased awareness of the responsibility of the individual conscience has introduced a flexibility into the nature of religious commitment. No longer are commitments eternally binding; instead they can be re-evaluated, and are therefore rendered flexible. Belief in general is seen as a medium which one can spend, accumulate, or lose during the unfolding of one's life in the faith.

According to McCready, the Catholic Pentecostal movement arose because many people began to feel a need for some outside force to intervene in a "positive wish-fulfillment belief." In other words:

> People who were very involved in religious struggles on a personal and professional level felt unable to exert any real influence on the direction in which the Church was moving. A "wish" began to emerge that another answer appear. The Third Person of the Trinity (Holy Spirit) had acquired a reputation over the years for curiosity into human affairs, and thus provided a ready supplier of answers. Several people of like minds and needs happened to meet and a contagious spreading of wish-fulfillment began.

What will be the direction of the Catholic church in the future? In the opinion of Hans Kung: "It is practically impossible to imagine how the Church will look in ten years." No one knows exactly how the church will overcome the crises it faces, but one force may help. It is what the theologian calls "the strength of faith."

CHAPTER TEN

During Sabbath services at a
Cleveland, Ohio, synagogue,
a member of the congregation
is called to read the day's text
while the rabbi points out
the lines.

The Synagogue Will Survive

Judaism means tradition, many thousands of years of it. It means legend. But it also means independence of mind and spirit. Thus, in many influential Jewish quarters the protest of young Jews against the traditional synagogue is seen as a healthy sign, as an affirmation rather than a condemnation of faith.

Reform Rabbi Alexander M. Schindler, vice president of The Union of American Hebrew Congregations, offers this view of the protest by the young:

> Of course they (the youth) are rebels and they rebel against religion too, but only as it is narrowly, mistakenly conceived. They reject institutionalism with its swollen pride and its divisiveness. They disdain all formalism, the clinging to cere-monial prayers on state occasions, invocations at football games, the bland recitation of doctrine which lacks all fire in the belly. But they do not reject the concept of human worth. They hold life sacred. They speak of man's relation-ship to man and really mean it. They insist that all cannot be chaos, that life must yield its meaning, and they persist in the quest to discover that meaning.

Thus, Rabbi Schindler believes the moving away from reli-gion is, paradoxically, a moving towards it, a reaching for the essence of religion. Man yearns for inwardness, he says. It is not enough to accumulate knowledge; modern man needs a sense of awe. He notes:

161

Many of our young people are even drawn to religious mysticism . . . they submit themselves to disciplines designed to refine man's sense of inwardness. Chassidism has made its mark among them. More than a few of our sons, the products of Reform religious education, now wear yarmulkes (skullcaps), eat only kosher food, and say their prayers—say them daily, mind you—wrapped in a tallis (prayer shawl). . . . The preoccupation with eastern religions also continues, on the campus and off, and many young Jews are among such seekers.

One of Judaism's most eminent spokesmen, Rabbi Abraham J. Heschel, has a similar view of the dissatisfied youth. In an interview with the editors of this book, he said:

I consider the present young generation to be a generation of hunger and quest, disenchanted with the superficialities and pragmatism of the older generation. There is a craving, there is a waiting, there is a searching. What are they looking for? First of all, they are looking for spontaneity. Secondly they are looking for community, fellowship. Traditionally Jews lived in small communities and small fellowships. Now the masses go to the synagogue, and there is no fellowship or very little. And thirdly, I would say that the young people have been eliminated completely from the working of the synagogue—the synagogue is overly concerned with what the older people have to say and to offer. There is a sort of patronizing attitude toward the young; they are occasionally given a little honor to be *bar mitzvahed*. But they are never asked to give an opinion and they have no participation. Obviously it is healthy and marvelous that the young people do want to speak out, to say what they feel and what they think.

Rabbi Heschel feels that youth are seeking "some kind of spiritual answer" to the problems they face. "How this will end," he says, "Whether it will end in something great and creative or whether it will peter out, remains to be seen. But the hunger is there. I am one hundred percent certain that there is a tremendous hunger for spiritual orientation."

Another who believes there is a deep undercurrent of faith in our time is Reform Rabbi Eugene Borowitz, professor of Jewish thought at the Manhattan campus of Hebrew Union

Rabbi Abraham J. Heschel, philosopher, theologian, and professor at the Jewish Theological Seminary in New York is a close observer of today's youth and one of Judaism's most eminent spokesmen.

College—Jewish Institute of Religion.

Rabbi Borowitz considers the current religious revival a major phenomenon, a startling turnabout from the "God is Dead" theology of the late 1960s. However, he cautions that movements need time to mature and often they are not given this time. In his opinion:

> Something is happening, but this something gets blown out of all proportion. And the participants themselves begin to feel that salvation is coming instantly. It is self-fulfilling. They cannot stand the idea that a movement may take ten or fifteen years to develop.

At the same time, Rabbi Borowitz sees a certain kind of Jewish activism that is different from the dissent taking place in other religions in America because Jewish spirituality is related to Jewish ethnic identity. Young Jews, he says, are asserting their Jewishness by discussing the state of Israel and the plight of Jews in the Soviet Union and by questioning many of the compromises and decisions made by the older generation. For example, says Rabbi Borowitz, they want to know where the charities go? Why more money doesn't go into Jewish education? And why so much is sent overseas?

Young Jews are also discussing what it means to be authentically Jewish. Today, according to Rabbi Borowitz, "We live in a time when the primary ideology of being a human being is existential, which is profoundly anti-institutional. So today's Jewish youth are existential Jews. They want not institutions, but community. They want communication that is person to person, face to face."

In this context, the synagogue as an institution has fallen subject to criticism. To understand the full why of this, however, it is necessary to understand how the synagogue's role has changed in history and how over the years American Jews have come to have different needs for the synagogue.

In the middle ages the synagogue was part of a disciplined Jewish community. Thus, it served as a place for Jewish community functions. It did not compete with other institutions for members. On the other hand, as more and more synagogues were built, especially in the western hemisphere, they began to compete with each other. Soon fraternal lodges began to take over many of the synagogue's functions, and as business and professional associations grew, the synagogues were no longer used as often for social activities.

Rabbi Eugene J. Lipman of Temple Sinai in Washington, D.C., gives this description of how the synagogue has changed in America:

> As American Jewry carried on its love affair with American culture, both public, organized religious activity (synagogue-based) and Jewish observances in the home became an increasingly occasional, ceremonial activity in the lives of our people. The vitality of the synagogue withered proportionately. In order to compete more effectively with other Jewish institutions, the synagogue, especially after 1920, undertook to become a synagogue-center, whether or not it called itself one. By bringing Jews into the building on any pretext, for any purpose however irrelevant, we hoped somehow to sneak some Torah into them, perhaps by osmosis. Sisterhoods developed—synagogue ladies' clubs. Brotherhoods developed—poker games gradually superseded by football star-studded father-son dinners. When parents of Jewish teenagers became sufficiently frightened of expanding non-Jewish social relationships, youth groups developed.

Rabbi Lipman feels that too many Jews attend the synagogue only on High Holidays or when there is a family celebration or emergency. Many people, he says, are relaxed about being Jews only if the synagogue and Jewishness make few demands on them. Furthermore, he adds, "their children are justifiably bored with us, and when they leave home, they want no part of our institutional irrelevancies."

Along with these difficulties, Rabbi Lipman believes a leadership problem exists in the American synagogue:

> The congregational rabbi cannot exercise much leadership, because the concerns of his institution's leaders have little to do with him, with his ordained purposes, with his concept of Judaism. Institutional survival is on their minds, and whatever the rabbi does must have survival value. Rabbis cannot teach much Judaism, because there are so few people around

to teach it to—they are not in our classrooms, they are not in adult seminars, they are not in the synagogue when sermons are preached. So the rabbi contents himself with minority loneliness, or he seeks out the irrelevant and tries to convince himself that it's the rabbinical necessity.

What should the response to these challenges be? Some Jewish leaders believe the structure of the synagogue should be changed. Rabbi Schindler, for example, believes that a de-emphasis of form, a greater flexibility, and a softening of rigidity is needed. In his opinion:

The synagogue building itself will have to become less big, less fixed, more modular for the mobile age. . . . The barrier between the pulpit and the pew must be broken down. We must de-professionalize religious life. More laymen must be brought into the decision-making process of the congregation, and not just on an administrative level but its substantive concerns as well. The hierarchical order of temple life is obsolete. Religious leadership must function, can function only in other than top-down terms.

Rabbi Schindler warns, however, that one cannot expect this change to occur suddenly—as suddenly, for example, as the challenges that have been meted out—for to change so suddenly means running the risk of losing one's followers.

Another Jewish leader, Reform Rabbi Eugene Lipan, proposes that separate, independently-operated synagogues give way to a single administrative unity within a large community and that this single unit then allow small groups "organized as they wish to be organized to do their Jewish thing." These small groups, operating within the Reform Jewish community umbrella, would work on special projects such as social action programs and would thereby counter the formality and fixed structure of the large centralized institution.

Rabbi Lipman would also set standards for membership in the Reform Jewish community. They include the following rules:

Let no one be retained in our membership who does not join a small group and participate in its serious study and work.

Let there be no child in a Reform religious school whose parents do not study Judaism. Let there be no further vacu-umized Reform religious education which is not education at all because the children come from and live in essentially non-Jewish homes, in which there is no Jewish function, feel, atmosphere, reality.

Although most Jewish leaders admit that there is a great deal of truth to the charge that the traditional synagogue has not responded to contemporary needs, many feel it is time to call a moratorium on such criticism. For example, Rabbi Balfour Brickner, Director of the Commission on Interfaith Activities of the Union of American Hebrew Congregations, points out that synagogues are still a reality and that they will continue to be so. First, he says, "they are the primary if not the sole agency in American Jewish life with which Jewish adults iden-tify Jewishly as they sink roots in a community. The search for, if not the assertion of, Jewish identity has never been more in vogue in America than it is now."

Rabbi Brickner believes that the synagogue will survive be-cause adults will always desire to give their children a religious education and an identity with their history. So the question then, he says, is not whether the synagogue is a relic but rather "how to transform it into a more meaningful, creative and a more responsive reality."

In the *Jewish Spectator,* Rabbi Brickner asserted:

There are still viable possibilities for the synagogue. It still commands huge reservoirs of respect and power which, if it ceases to be timid and stops being all things to all people, can become vital again. It will mean that the synagogue will have to budget as much money for programs as for building maintenance. It means social action and interreligious affairs involvement. It means pushing the congregation into urban renewal and housing and Minority Economic Small Business Investment Corporation. It means turning back to work with the larger community, Christian, black, and secular. . . .

According to Rabbi Brickner, the latest Jewish syndrome is a tendency to withdraw from significant involvement in social concerns of the community. He emphasizes that Jews "need to resist the temptation to withdraw in self-isolation . . . we must reassert our traditional Jewish willingness to take risks. . . . It means working for human rights, tolerating the unlike and defending another's difference even when he curses you. It means using the Jewish institutions and agencies, the Jewish community and the synagogue, in new and different ways—and not simply writing them off."

Others join in the view that the synagogue in America will survive. Conservative Rabbi Wolfe Kelman, for instance, executive vice-president of the Rabbinical Assembly, said recently that American religious life has reached a point of consolidation. In his words:

> The period of synagogal growth is over, but this does not mean that the synagogue or Judaism in America is dead or dying. The apathy of American Jews toward their Judaism no longer exists; our Jews are no longer indifferent to their religious heritage. Instead, there is a hunger for Jewish understanding and education that, while different from that of the past, is nevertheless significant and valid today.

No one will deny, however, that one of the foundations of the Jewish community in the United States, the urban synagogue, is floundering as more and more people move to the suburbs. Nor will many deny that Jewish educators are facing a dilemma. The old cultural climate in which Jews gained a strong sense of Jewish identity has been so weakened that many young Jews shrug off their Jewishness. Their parents when young may have had some contact with the old ghetto community in Europe but the young of today have had no primary contact with Jewish language and symbols. And without this organic community the Jewish classroom, as James A. Sleeper writes in *The New Jews*, "is charged with the impossible responsibility of providing emotional attachment to Jewishness, and with setting up a socializing area in which Jewish 'values' may be acted out, Jewish symbols employed as natural reflexes to the broad spectrum of a day's activities and secret moments."

Somehow, Sleeper adds, "the Jewish school is expected to

'reach out' to the essentially non-Jewish student, in a language foreign to the tradition, across a widening cultural and philosophical chasm. It is doubtful that even the most extravagantly budgeted and hardwared classroom can do these things."

He quotes a girl in a confirmation class as saying, "My life is too rich and beautiful for Judaism," and then responds himself by saying, "What is sad is that the things which do make her life 'rich and beautiful' are so meager and threadbare in comparison to the riches of Jewishness; yet they are grasped and held so strongly because they are personal and real, something Judaism is not."

Sleeper sees the *havurot* (see Chapter 6) as an attempt to create an organic Jewish community and says because their members "embrace youth culture in order to transform it, they are excellent meeting points between the young and the tradition."

On the other hand the quest for meaning that has accompanied the new forms of worship has raised numerous questions. For example, how much of what is going on is religion? Is the quest for meaning automatically "religious"?

Rabbi Alfred Jospe of the Hillel Foundations made this comment, "Reading poetry or singing folk songs on a Friday evening may be a beautifully satisfying aesthetic and emotional experience. But does it constitute authentic worship even when it takes place on *erev Shabbat*?"

Rabbi Jospe urges caution about any form of worship in which the participants "speak only of themselves and describe their private emotions, beautiful, touching, and moving as they may be, without relating them to a search for or awareness of an ultimate." What is missing in some of the experimental services, he says, is "a quest for or sense of an ultimate reality beyond ourselves, no matter what name we give to it. In short, the question is whether the verbalization of private emotions can and should be defined as worship regardless of its intent and content."

Rabbi Jospe further asks, "To what extent and in what ways can this kind of worship be defined as Jewish?"

By posing this question, he is noting that to be Jewish involves the use of symbols, rituals, observances, celebrations and a sense of history. The new kinds of private prayers uttered in experimental services, he believes, conceivably could also be said by a Hindu, Christian, or Buddhist. And if the Jewish tradition of continuity is lost the rabbi wonders, if self-exploration does not necessarily emerge out of a sense of the past but if it emerges instead out of a sense of self, what links these new Jews to the "time dimension" of Jewish experience?

Still despite their doubts about the direction young Jews are taking in their search for new forms of worship, many Jewish leaders believe their quest is to some extent justified.

In his book *Man's Quest for God*, Rabbi Heschel expresses a similar discontent with the atmosphere of today's synagogue:

> The modern temple suffers from a severe cold. Congregations preserve a respectful distance between the liturgy and

themselves. They say the words, "Forgive us for we have sinned," but of course, they are not meant. They say, "Thou shalt love the Lord Thy God with all thy heart . . ." in lofty detachment, in complete anonymity as if giving an impartial opinion about an irrelevant question.

An air of tranquility, complacency prevails in our house of worship. What can come out of such an atmosphere? The services are prim, the voice is dry, the temple is clean and tidy, and the soul of prayer lies in agony. You know no one will scream, no one will cry, the words will be stillborn . . . if prayer is as precious a deed as an act of charity, we must stop being embarrassed at our saying Praised be Thou with inner devotion.

CHAPTER ELEVEN

The Outlook for Religion

Predictions are always in danger. In the nineteenth century, for instance, many observers predicted that as man developed more rational modes of thought, religion would decline and eventually disappear as a strong force. According to this argument, religion was the result of ignorance and superstition, and the more educated and enlightened man became the less he would "need" it.

This of course has not happened. Religion has flourished in American society, which is the most advanced on earth, and, as this book has shown, it is a source of widespread and increasing interest among great numbers of young people.

Today the world is in a constant state of flux. Technological innovation is all around us. There is change everywhere, undermining man's feeling of stability and permanence. Human relationships are not as lasting as they used to be. People meet more people, and the friendships which result do not always have time to develop fully; there are commuter friends, golf friends, work friends, and hundreds of other transient relationships that arise from the mobile world in which we live.

Thereupon rests a good case for the future of religion. If futurologists are to be believed, the greater the pace of acceleration becomes, the more man will need the permanence of religion. There may be glorious times ahead in this "belle epoque," this age of progress, says Herman Kahn, director of the Hudson Institute in Croton, New York. But man's "biggest problem," he observes, is religious. Speaking before the First White House Conference on the Industrial World, held in February, 1972, he declared, "The biggest single problem facing us is meaning and purpose. Why do we stay alive? What are we here for? My grandfather walked with God and knew why, but we don't."

"We are becoming more successful, so increasingly we're going to have the failure of success, because of rising expectations," Kahn told some 1,500 corporation executives. This "increasing disillusionment with progress," could become part of a "1985 technological crisis," he warned, noting that "about 100 bad things could happen" around the year 1985. "The odds against any one happening are about 100 to 1," he said. "But if you have 100 of them, the chances are good that one will."

Consider, then, the dangers of environmental disaster and the possibility, however remote, of the technological control of man in this scientific age, and you have further cause to believe in the future of religion.

We will take a look at some interesting predictions about what may happen to religion in the future, but first let us look at some things that are not expected to happen.

Catholic sociologist Andrew M. Greeley, Program Director for Higher Education at the University of Chicago's National Opinion Research Center, sets forth four interesting "nots" in his book *Religion in the Year 2000*.

Organized churches will not lose their members, he says. "In the United States this means that membership, church attendance, and doctrinal orthodoxy will persist at the levels reported in the 1952-1965 surveys. In countries such as England where organized participation and church attendance levels are much lower, this means minimally that levels are likely to fall no lower than they are, and . . . may begin to rise slightly."

For the vast majority of people, Father Greeley believes, religion will not lose its "influence," nor will the secular replace the sacred. He notes: "Scientific rationalism will not generate a new faith. On the contrary, in fact, the popularity of the current revolt against scientific rationalism suggests that new and deviant forms of the sacred will emerge."

174

Furthermore, despite the ecumenical movement, Father Greeley predicts that the Western religious scene will continue to be characterized by denominations. On the other hand, he believes that numerous drastic changes will take place, including a growing dialogue between religion and the social sciences and a greater understanding of what religious traditions outside of Christianity have to offer. He concludes by writing:

> What we are predicting, then is that in the next 30 to 50—even 100—years we will not witness the rapid, or even the gradual evolution, but rather the slow evolution of religion. Of course it is possible that the whole process of human history has been so shaken in the last half century that the projection of trends in the future, on the basis of the past and the present, is no longer valid. It may be that one can no longer assert that just as religion has evolved into the present, so it will continue to evolve into the future, perhaps at an accelerated rate. Furthermore, even though religion has outlived all those who prophesied its doom in the past, it may be that the human condition has changed so much that this time the prophets of doom are correct.

Other observers of the religious scene would disagree with some of Father Greeley's predictions. For example, Dr. Gerald J. Jud, General Secretary of the Division of Evangelism of the United Church of Christ, believes denominationalism is dying. "There really is no biblical basis or good common-sense reason to keep it alive in our kind of world," he says. "Denominationalism served a purpose in its time, but it has fulfilled its function and now deserves a dignified death. Already there are . . . many clusters of churches (that are) joining their resources in planning for participation in God's mission in their areas and beyond."

Dr. Jud also predicts that the leadership in the local churches is changing, developing toward a "style that is open and vulnerable, a style that does not presume to have all of the answers or the last word." He calls this a "helping alongside" style and says that as it emerges pastors will gain a new sense of confidence. They will "see their function essentially as bearers of the historical tradition (specialists in biblical theology), trained helpers of people with personal problems, experts in the field of communications, and group therapy specialists in worship."

Theologian Harvey Cox of the Harvard Divinity School, while acknowledging that "the seer's job is always a precarious one," made the following predictions at a Conference on Religion and the Future, sponsored by the Lancaster (Pennsylvania) Theological Seminary, the United Church of Christ, Crozer Theological Seminary, and the American Baptist Convention. His remarks subsequently appeared in *The Futurist* magazine:

1. Denominational Christianity, organized into national bodies with state and local "distributors" will certainly disappear. The disputes that separated Baptists from Presbyterians, and Episcopalians from Methodists are simply not that interesting to anyone anymore. Also, the whole idea of nationally organized denominations, modeled after nationwide corporations, is not suited to emerging religious ethos with its emphasis on universality and intimacy. This does not mean that particular strands of Christianity will not endure. I think they will, but in greatly transmuted form.

2. Each person will more and more assemble his own "collage" or personal symbol system, made up of elements from various systems that give shape to his own life. . . . The collage-building will be done at the individual, not the institutional level. And the collage, although it will borrow from various traditions, just as many Catholics now practice Zen meditation, will still be recognizably shaped by one predominant tradition. Maybe these personal religious styles would have to be called "Christianoid" or "Judaoid" rather than Christian or Jewish for example, but the identifiable shape and the continuity with the larger tradition will be there.

3. In all religious traditions, the "dionysiac" element marked by ecstasy, joy, emotion, and movement will certainly reassert itself as against the dominant "apollonian" element of the present. This tendency can already be seen in the fascination for dance, beads, bodily awareness, ritual movement and color which characterize the religious aspects of the youth culture today.

4. We will see a further reaching out for exotic symbols of the transcendent. Ours is a culture in which people feel

hemmed in and constricted. Samuel Beckett depicts it in his play, *Happy Days,* where the characters sit in piles of sand up to their necks. Our feeling of being trapped also expresses itself in such street idioms as "in a rut," "on a dead-end street," or "hung-up." Man needs symbols of transcendence in order to remain open to life and fully human. But the symbols provided them by their cultures invariably suffer from domestication. They are detranscendentalized. . . . Consequently man is driven to reach further and further out (up?, down?) for symbols of transcendence which were previously taboo or not widely known. This is what has already happened with the Age of Aquarius. It also explains some of the current interest in such psychic sciences as Tarot cards, palmistry, astrology, and numerology. We can look for more of this in the future. . . .

At the same conference, professional futurologist, Herman Kahn predicted that in the future problems increasingly will be theological rather than technological. Other delegates expressed surprise that technological change is occurring so rapidly. Among them was Jesse H. Brown, a professor of Old Testament at Crozer Theological Seminary, who remarked:

> I think I have kept up moderately well with many of these technological changes and I feel I have some awareness of the trends in futurology, but I was still overwhelmed by the pace of change as revealed by many of the Conference leaders. What will this pace of change mean for those who are not so well informed? What additional responsibility do we have if the questions are increasingly more theological rather than technological? If it is the case that our future will change more rapidly than even the best informed can adequately anticipate, what is our responsibility for helping to interpret the mood and attitude of change in order to bring about more readiness and adaptability to change.

Whenever the future of religion is discussed, the effects of technological change are always debated. A key word that arises in this discussion is secularization, which, simply defined, means to put everything in terms of human disposition and scientific analysis. Or as theologian Harvey Cox has defined it:

177

> Secularization is the loosening of the world from religious and quasi-religious understandings of itself, the dispelling of all closed world views, the breaking of all supernatural myths and sacred symbols. It represents what another observer has called the "defatalization of history", the discovery by man that he has been left with the world on his hands, and that he can no longer blame fortune or the furies for what he does with it. Secularization is man turning his attention away from from worlds beyond and toward this world and this time. It is what Dietrich Bonhoeffer in 1944 called "man's coming of age."

Thus, secularism means that beliefs which were once considered inviolable and unquestionable are increasingly being examined and in some cases discarded. There is less need, many people think, for transcendent laws. Such questions as why can't man govern himself and why can't man get all of the goals and standards he needs from his own social and natural environments are being asked with greater frequency. In their book, *The Year 2000*, Herman Kahn and Anthony J. Wiener call this an increasingly secular, humanistic, and pragmatic long-term trend and claim that it poses a major challenge for the church.

Lutheran sociologist Peter L. Berger offered a similar view in the Methodist magazine *World Outlook*. Writing about religion in the year 2000, he observed that:

> Secularization will continue. If one means by religion a belief in God and a relationship to God, then I think there will be less of this, fewer "religious people" in this sense. Secularization is a process by which this happens, that religion to "religious people" becomes less real. Religion and religious entities lose their reality to people. . . . People become closed to reality and to aspects of their own experience. There is a trivialization of mystery, or ecstasy, and of awe, and a resulting impoverishment, from a Christian point of view.

But he added, there is a good side to secularization because the "structure of religious belief can no longer be taken for granted." In Berger's opinion: "Secularization forces people to

make choices and makes for a better situation in which to con-
front the religious options clearly."

On the other hand, many observers of the religious scene
today believe the church will be more important in the year
2000 than it is now. For example, J. Edward Carothers, Associate General Secretary of the United Methodist Church's
Board of Missions, made this prediction in the Board's magazine *World Outlook*:

> Man's real problem is his sanity, his sense of meaning, his
> reason for enduring the things in life over which he has no
> control—or only marginal control. This includes growing
> older, pain of body and mind, disappointments in love and
> friendship, betrayals of himself or others, the creeping in of
> old age and inevitable death; and there are many more, as
> Ecclesiastes takes partial note. In the year 2000 these issues
> will be more pressing. As physical existence becomes easier,
> spiritual existence attracts more of our concern, and prob-
> lems we would not otherwise have time or energy to think
> about become very important to us. In 2000 we will have a
> lot more to ponder plus more distraction opportunities than
> are good for us. Our deep apprehensions about the meaning
> of life will have to be answered in a world where everybody
> believes in the evolutionary nature of things and has also ar-
> rived at a point where existence is more perplexed by unor-
> ganized knowledge than it is by the realms of the unknown.

On a more specific level, for instance in the Catholic
church, there are predictions that priests may become "union-
ized." According to Jesuit priest Father John C. Haughey, the
time will come when groups of priests, acting on both local
and national levels, will take this step to give the priesthood its
full due. In an article for the Jesuit magazine *America*, he
made the following predictions about the church in the 1970s:

> By the middle of the decade a new and volatile element
> will have entered the staid galaxy of ecclesiastical authority:
> the priest's wife. The Roman Catholic Church will decide to
> make clerical celibacy optional. The consequences will be
> many—not least of which will be a new respect for mar-
> riage, an increase in the number of priests and an enhanced
> dignity for the celibate vocation. . . .

What else can Catholics look for? In the field of education wrote Father Neil G. McCluskey of Gonzaga University: "Look for the demise of many Catholic colleges, as such, some of which will have deserved a better fate. Look for a radically less dominant role of the founding religious group and new relationships to the various publics the institution serves through its governance, accountability and support."

Father McCluskey also noted that hundreds of elementary and secondary schools have been forced to close due to a lack of funds and a shortage of teaching nuns and observed: "It is no secret that each of the last five years has seen several thousand religious women departing their convents and a diminishing flow of recruits entering religious life to replace them."

In many cases, lay teachers have been hired to replace nuns, but their cost is estimated to be four to six times that of the nuns—spurring a national move to make state funds available for parochial schools. As one Catholic educator put it, "Unless the federal government and the state governments come forward with more aid, we cannot survive."

The high cost of maintaining religious establishments is contributing to another trend in communities throughout the United States. In the planned community of Columbia, Maryland, for example, a single religious edifice is used for religious services of all faiths. Protestants for example, might use the structure on Sunday morning, Catholics on Sunday afternoon, and Jews on Friday evening. Some congregations have gone a step further. In one New England town Congregationalists and Methodists merged their services, thereby saving the salary of one minister. And in another instance, Presbyterians and Jews have shared family counseling services and joined together to work with retarded children.

Incidents such as these prompted one sociologist, Daniel M. Schores of Austin College in Texas, to state that a "coordinated ecumenical approach" will help determine the shape of the world in the year 2000. This type of ministry he has said, will demand "not compromises for the sake of harmony or public relations, but complete abandonment of denominational approaches in favor of a concentrated attack by all Christians on the problems of our times, marked by mutual trust and openness."

Furthermore, within the next thirty years, said Schores, new construction in America will total as much as has been built from 1776 to now and "no denomination can afford separate church buildings if adequate service is to be provided."

In an article for *The Futurist* magazine, Schores suggested that modern technology could be put to wise use by the churches in the twenty-first century. Imagine home services for shut-ins via closed circuit TV or the use of television for simultaneous worship services, he said. Think what a library of tapes might do for membership training courses or church history presentations or social issues workshops. Consider how "talking typewriters" or information screens from ecumenical learning centers could teach the Bible to high school students at their own paces. Imagine one computer linked by telephone lines to a thousand churches, providing automatic print-out notices of meetings and financial analysis of donations.

In the same article Schores proposed that clergymen devise "realistic, perhaps computer-simulated, models or situations likely to be encountered by prospective clergy." Furthermore, he said, clergymen should "dream up new shapes for ministry —in seminary think-tanks parallel to those of space-age industries. I would like to introduce seminarians to futuristic designs for floating cities, under-the-sea mining communities, and moon villages and challenge them to think through viable alternatives for ministry. More field experience, less reliance upon traditional content, televised lectures by famous scholars, increased familiarity with research methods, less memorizing of soon out-dated information, required return to formal schooling by use of sabbatical years—these are my suggestions to my colleagues."

Of course much of the future of religion depends on what is still to be discovered. Futurologist T. J. Gordon, Senior Research Fellow at the Institute for the Future in Middletown, Connecticut, asks us to consider what might happen if extraterrestial life is discovered. In remarks before the Conference on Religion and the Future, published in the journal *The Futurist*, he asserted:

> Just as surely as Copernicus removed the earth from the
> center of the solar system, such a discovery would dramati-
> cally complete the process of removing man's ego from the
> center of the universe. No longer would we be giant mole-
> cules scurrying ant-like without purpose on an indistin-
> guished planet circling a pedestrian star in an ordinary gal-
> axy. We would be members of a community of life,
> participants in a drama bigger than we could have dreamed.
> And, if we can exchange information with our distant con-
> temporaries, we will surely ask, "What of God?"

Researcher Gordon also points out that at least two other
areas of radical change are likely to continue affecting the
church. The first relates to the role of social action:

> We are no longer surprised by clergymen participating in
> civil rights picket lines or protest demonstrations, priests
> challenging the dogma of institutions they consider outmod-
> ed—including their own—or ministers supporting itinerant
> workers striking for better conditions of employment . . .
> this new force from the church seems to be particularly vir-
> ile. It carries authority, appears less parochial than other
> special interest groups, and brings new vitality to issues that
> promise to be central in the next few decades.

The second area of radical change is the church's role in establishing guidelines for moral behavior:

> Less than ever before, it seems, do values of society stem di-
> rectly from the church. People now follow other drummers.
> To be sure, today's value systems are being built on the base
> laid by Judeo-Christian principles, but what dimensions will
> they assume in the future and what will be the Church's re-
> sponse to these unfamiliar modes which grow from new
> technology and popular ideologies? What will be its re-
> sponse, for example, to new forms of marriage contracts,
> which might include no marriage, trial marriage, group mar-
> riage, or homosexual marriage? Or to the general acceptance
> of the view that sexual enjoyment is distinct from love and
> from the reproductive process? Such an attitude is almost
> here now. . . .

Thus, the future of religion depends on the answers to many questions. For example: What part will Christianity play among the emerging people of the Third World—Africa, Asia and Latin America? Will the church remain an authoritative teacher for laymen and priests? Will Christianity itself survive, that is Christianity as we now know it? Will science and technology dominate all aspects of life? Will there be a future world utopian community? What if today's pollution and racial problems are not solved? What if man searches but fails to find other intelligent beings? What will his response be? What if science fails society? What if the occult and the mystical replace some conventional denominations? Will religious institutions always dictate morals? If intelligent beings are found in the universe, should man try to convert them? Will drugs or new psychological techniques give rise to an "experiential" theology in which man's mind and imagination will conjure up new kinds of reality?

And so on and on go the questions. The local church is expected to remain, as a place to baptize babies, to confirm and educate members, and to act as a center for the public worship of God. But the problem of the future remains. There is great concern in the religious community about the future.

But after all is said and done, who can really predict the future of religion—or the future of anything? Perhaps the wisest and profoundest thing that can be said on the subject simply is, "Only God knows."

Index

actualism, 92
Adopt-a-Building, 134
adult education, 147, 148
affluence, Jesus people and, 44
Agape (commune), 35
Age of Aquarius, 85-86
Agus, Robert, 97
Ahmadiyya Movement, 118-119
alchemy, 92
alienation, Jewish dissent, 104
American Baptist Convention, 114
American Baptist Service Corporation, 134
American Council of Learned Societies, 16
American overseas, Children of God and, 38-39
Aquarian Agent (magazine), 83
Aquarian University of Maryland (Baltimore, Maryland), 86
asceticism, Eastern religions, 67
astrology, 81-82, 83
authority:
    Catholic Church and, 144, 155
    Catholic dissent, 142-143
    church self-confidence, 131-132
awe. see reverence

B

Baba communities, 74
Back to Africa Movement, 114
bakhti Yoga, 64, 75
Baltimore, Maryland, 86
baptism of the Spirit, 55, 56
Baptist churches, black, 111
Bartell, Ernest, 150
Berger, Peter L., 131, 178-179
Beverly Hills, California, 137
Bhaktivedanta Swami, A. C., 64
Bible:
    Jesus Movement and, 126
    New Testament, Gospels, 40-41, 158
    New Testament, Matthew, 40

Bible (continued)
    study of, 16, 26, 28
bishops and priests, 144, 153-154
black caucuses, 111
Black (Satanic) magic, 88
Black Muslims, 117-118
blacks, 107-120, 134
Blessitt, Arthur, 34
B'nai B'rith Hillel Foundations, 100, 104
Book of Changes. see I Ching
books, interest in occult, 82
Borowitz, Eugene, 162-164
Boston Havurat Shalom Community Seminary, 101
Boyd, Malcolm, 126
Brickner, Balfour, 167
Buddhism, 71-73, 75
buildingless synagogue, 100-101
business, "Jesus watch," exploitation?, 26-27
Byrd, Jean (Mrs.), 85

C

COG. see Children of God
California, 82, 139
Campus Crusade for Christ, 15
Campus ministry. see universities and college
Catholic Church:
    church attendance, 17
    in future, 179
    pentecostalism, 47-62
    unchangeable church?, 141-159
Catholic schools. see parochial schools
Catholic University of America (Washington, D. C.), 48-49, 151
Cayce, Edgar, 82
celibacy, Catholic Church, 156
change:
    Catholic Church, 141-159
    future shock and, 20
    theology and technology, 177

PHOTO CREDITS

U.S.News & World Report
  Warren K. Leffler—14
  Robin Megibow—33
Charles A. Blahusch—46,59,152
B'nai B'rith—160
Paul Conklin—38,122
Fabrangen of Washington—94,99
Robert Halvey—54,57,149
Home Board Photo—135
Magnum—24
Magnum, Bill Stanton—172
Magnum, Burk Uzzle—113
George Pickow—169
John H. Popper—163
Don Rutledge—62,80
Wide World Photos—19,30,70,76,106,138,140,145
UPI—106,146